Illustrator
Ken Tunell

Editor
Mara Ellen Guckian

Editorial Project Manager
Ina Massler Levin, M.A.

Editor in Chief
Sharon Coan, M.S. Ed.

Creative Director
Elayne Roberts

Art Coordinator
Denice Adorno

Cover Artist
Denise Bauer

Product Manager
Phil Garcia

Imaging
Ralph Olmedo, Jr.

Publishers
Rachelle Cracchiolo, M.S. Ed.
Mary Dupuy Smith, M.S. Ed.

P9-DFI-304

Big & Easy Patterns

Holidays & Seasons

Compiled by

Loralyn Radcliffe

Teacher Created Materials

Teacher Created Materials, Inc.
6421 Industry Way
Westminster, CA 92683
www.teachercreated.com

©2000 Teacher Created Materials, Inc.
Reprinted, 2000
Made in U.S.A.
ISBN-1-57690-602-7

Table of Contents

372.5
Holi

Table of Contents

Table of Contents

Using the Patterns

There are several ways to use the patterns in this book. The pieces are big and easy to cut out and assemble. They can be used by students as well as teachers. Reduce or enlarge them to fit your needs. Try to laminate pieces you will be placing in your centers.

Color-and-Cut Figures and Paper Sculpture

For an easy-to-prepare art project, simply reproduce the patterns on white construction paper, and have children color, cut out, and glue the pieces together at the tabs so that the finished product looks like the diagram. If the pattern would benefit from moving parts, try using brads instead of glue.

To make a stuffed paper sculpture, trace the outline of the assembled figure onto another blank piece of paper, decorate it, and cut it out. Put the two pieces together and staple them around the edges leaving one side open. Lightly stuff with crumpled newspaper, and then staple the opening shut.

Classroom Decorations and Story Prompts

The patterns can be used on bulletin boards, flannel boards, or magnetic boards. Copy the patterns on heavy stock, assemble, and then laminate them. Glue squares of felt or Velcro® to the back for use on the flannelboard, or attach the magnetic strips available at craft stores for magnetic board use. You can also hang the patterns from the ceiling with fishing line or use them to create mobiles. Use the patterns to generate class discussions about the various seasons and holidays and to spark ideas for story and journal writing.

Word Banks

A word bank is a collection of related words that grows as students learn more about the specific topic. Children gain ownership of the word bank as they add more words to the list. You can create a word bank for the fall with a basket of apples. Winter words can be gathered on snowflakes swirling around a snowman. Write letters, math facts, etc., right on the pattern. Use adhesive labels or white out to conceal design elements.

Puppets and Paper Dolls

Give each child a copy of a pattern to color, cut out, and glue to a craft stick for his or her own stick puppet. For a teacher set, use cardstock and laminate before gluing. You may wish to reduce the patterns or use the diagrams of fully assembled figures and enlarge to meet your needs, or make larger puppets. Attach the yardsticks or paint stirrers from the hardware store instead of craft sticks. Place a set of the laminated, colored patterns without craft sticks in the Drama Center for the students' use. Encourage the children to create their own dramas, and to make new clothes and accessories for the figures.

Big Books and Shape Books

Many of the patterns in this book lend themselves well to big books. Patterns can be used as covers, or they can be decorations for the inside pages. To make a big book, cut two pieces of poster board to the desired size and glue the colored pattern to one of the pieces. Punch holes down the side and bind all pages with yarn or rings. You can also make a large shape book by copying the pattern onto two pieces of cardstock for the front and back. Trim lined paper to fit inside the covers and bind the book with yarn, rings, or staples. Big books and shape books can be used for class-generated stories, poems, investigations, or reports, or they can be used as journals.

Fall Patterns and Ideas

Cut the windows out of the school bus and arrange photos of your students to look as if they are sitting in the bus. Use another copy of the same pattern to make a shape book entitled How We Get to School.

Use autumn leaves for patterning, sorting, or graphing activities, or to make a Fall Word Bank. Bring in a branch anchored in a large coffee can with sand or plaster of Paris and tie the leaves to the tree. Use the leaves as a countdown to an important date, removing one leaf each day; or mount student poems on enlarged leaves. Autumn leaves or acorns make great covers for fall journals too.

The acorn pattern can be used for math facts flash cards or as math manipulatives. Use the acorns with a squirrel pattern puppet to act out story problems, and leave a set in your math center for students to generate their own story problems with a partner. Use the squirrel, acorn, and owl patterns as puppets, and write fall animal facts on the acorns.

Christopher Columbus can be used as a story prop or puppet to relate to students his voyage to America. Write story events on copies of the ship pattern and let students use them as a sequencing activity.

Create a pumpkin math center. Record estimates of weight, height, and girth in a pumpkin book. Make a Halloween bulletin board using the spooky house, Jack O'Lantern, cat, bat, and spider patterns. Write spelling words on black bats with a white crayon or piece of chalk and suspend them from the ceiling with fishing line. Arrange thick yarn on the bulletin board in a spider-web shape. Collect spooky words, Halloween words, or spider words from your study on spiders and arrange the words around the spider web pattern.

Use the bat or cat pattern to create a class riddle book. Answers to the riddles should rhyme with "at." Each member of the class could contribute an illustrated page. Example: I sit on your head. I am a _____.

Make Pilgrim and Native American boys and girls by reproducing, coloring, and gluing pattern pieces to butcher paper. Use the boys and girls on the bulletin board or have students make stuffed paper sculptures. Place an enlarged *Mayflower* pattern on the bulletin board and decorate with waves made of blue crepe paper streamers.

Use the cornucopia to gather Thanksgiving words on the bulletin board or as an art project. The turkey pattern can be used as a paper sculpture, a cut-and-color craft, or a learning center game. Write math facts or questions about the pilgrim story on different colored feathers. Make a color-coded key for self-checking. Label turkeys with a numeral and write a math fact on each feather to correspond with

the numeral on the turkey. Have students sort the feathers and place them with the correct turkey. Make a similar game for phonics, by labeling each turkey with a letter from the alphabet and gluing or drawing pictures with the letter sounds on the feathers.

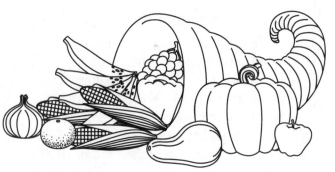

Ask the students how to prepare a turkey or to write about their favorite foods. Collect responses in a Turkey Dinner Shape Book.

Scarecrow

Use pages 7–9. Cut out and color all pieces. Connect the head to torso at Tab A. Connect the arms to torso at Tabs B & C. Connect the scarecrow feet to torso at Tabs D & E.

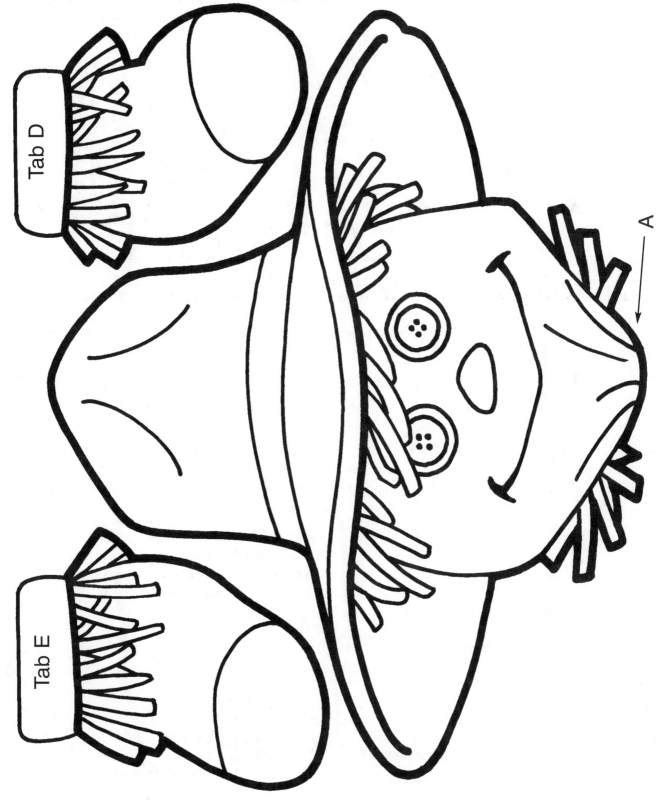

Scarecrow *(cont.)*

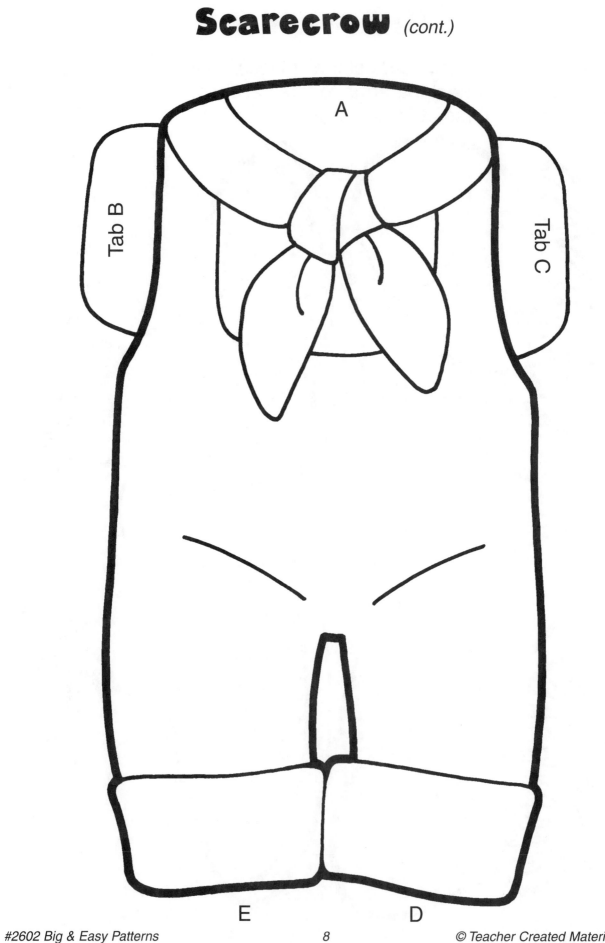

Scarecrow *(cont.)*

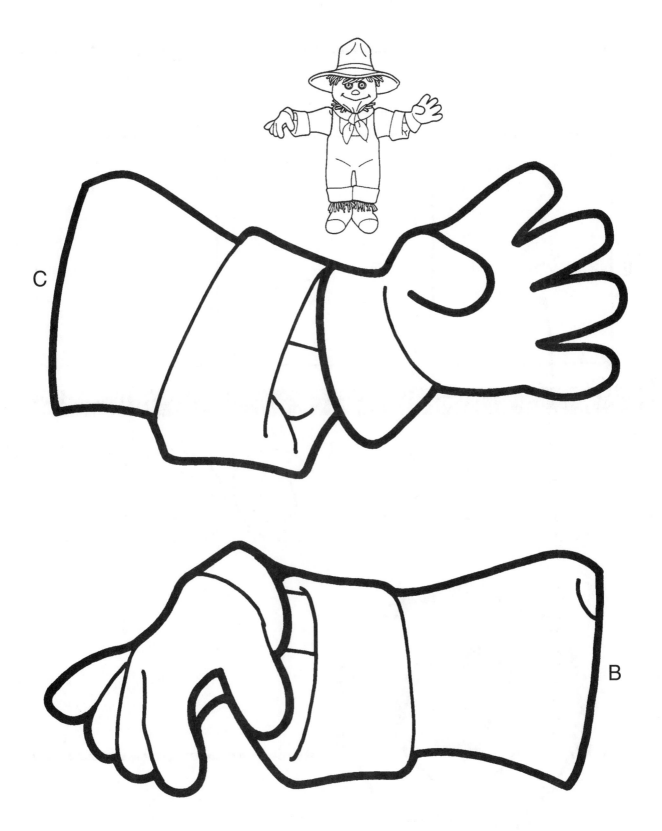

C

B

Fall

School Bus

Use pages 10–11. Connect the bus at the tab.

School Bus *(cont.)*

Tab

SCHOOL

Autumn Leaves

Maple

Autumn Leaves *(cont.)*

Oak

Autumn Leaves *(cont.)*

Poplar

14

Squirrel

Use pages 15–17. See page 16 for directions.

Squirrel *(cont.)*

Attach squirrel head to A.
Attach arms to either side
of paper at B.
Place acorn between
paws. Attach legs to
either side
of paper at D.
Attach the tail at C.

A

B

D

C

D

Squirrel *(cont.)*

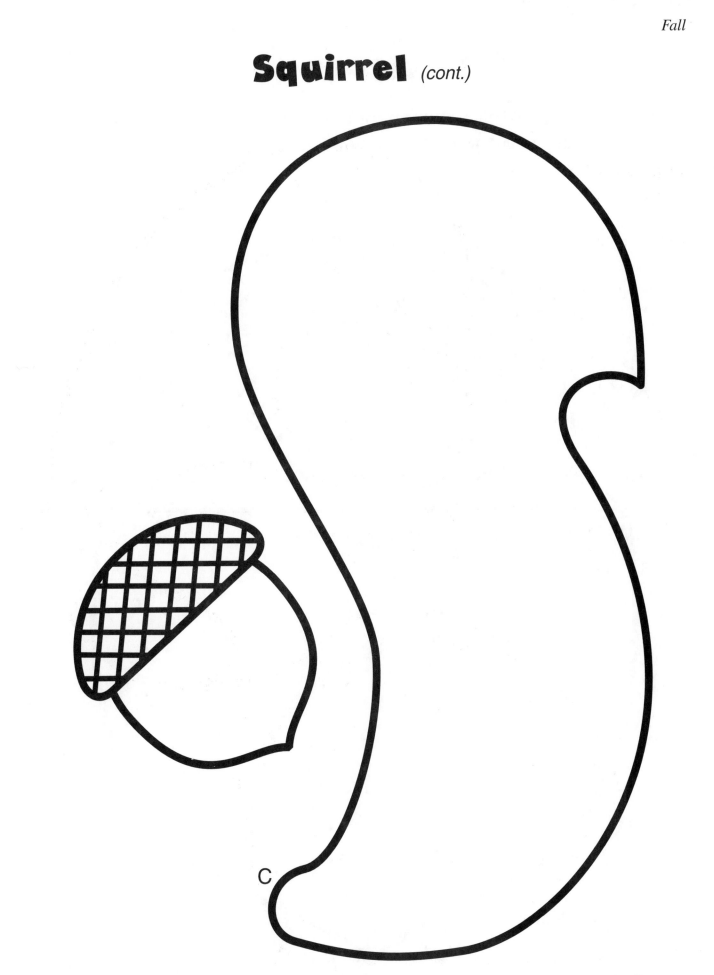

C

Fall

Acorn

Add lines to create fall stationery or enlarge to use as a journal cover. Duplicate pattern to create a word wall.

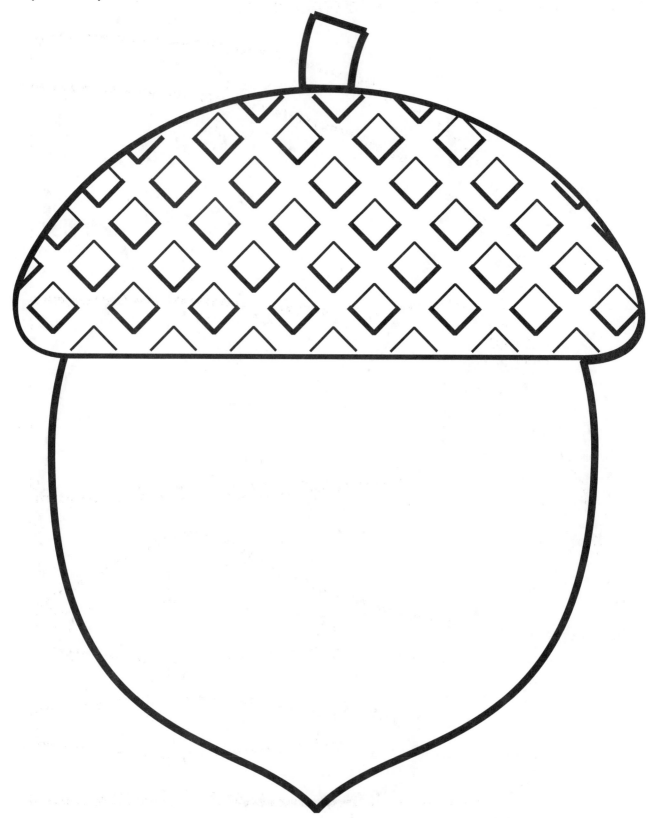

#2602 Big & Easy Patterns   18   © Teacher Created Materials, Inc.

Basket

Use pages 19–20. Cut out and color pieces. Connect the basket at the tab. Cut on the dotted line to open basket.

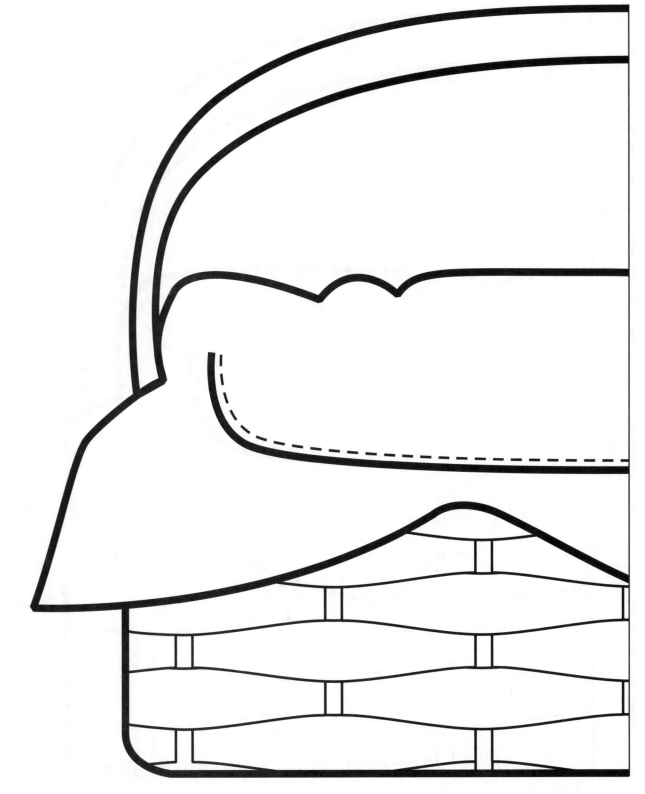

Basket *(cont.)*

Fill the basket with autumn leaves (pages 12–14), acorns (page 17), apples (page 21), or vegetables and fruits (pages 56–57).

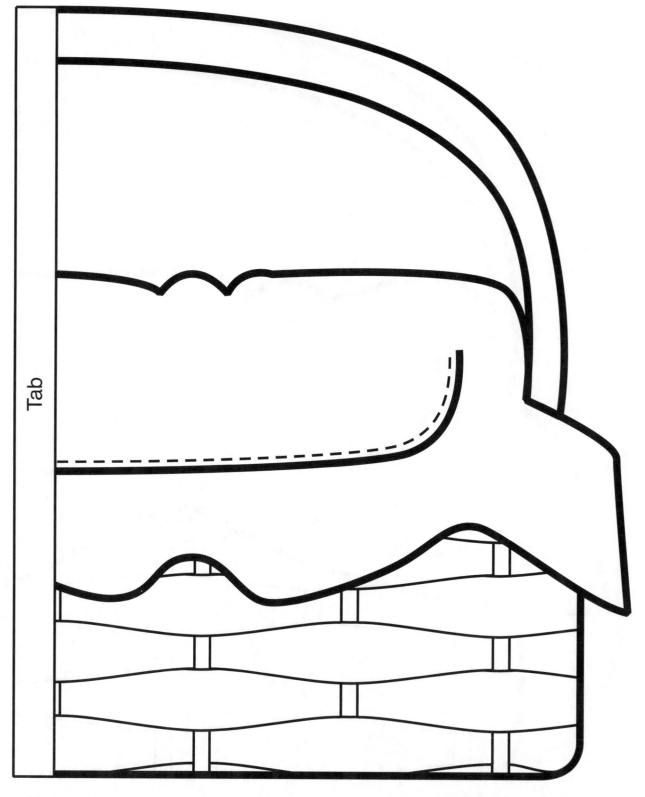

Apples

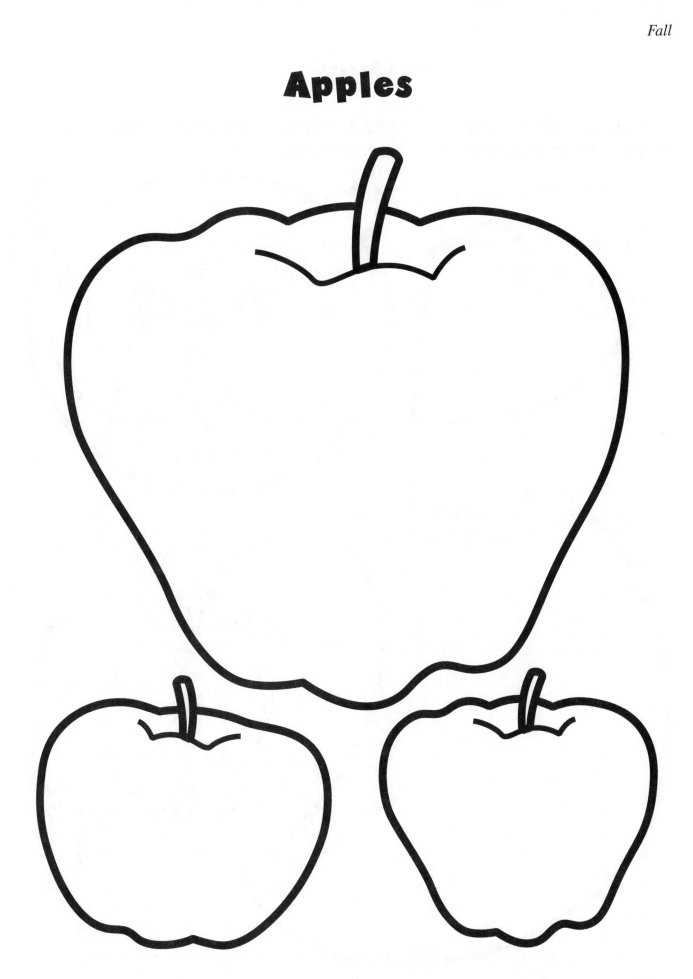

Owl

Use pages 22–23. Attach the head at Tab A and tail at Tab B. Coat breast with glue and sprinkle with birdseed.

Tail

Tab B

C

Tab A

Tab D

B

Owl *(cont.)*

Cut out wings and branch with talons. Glue sunflower seeds or small feathers to the wings and attach to the torso at Tabs C & D. Attach the branch and talons as shown in diagram.

Pumpkin

24

Christopher Columbus

Use pages 25–27. Attach the head to torso at Tab A. Attach the arm to torso at Tab B and legs to torso at Tab C.

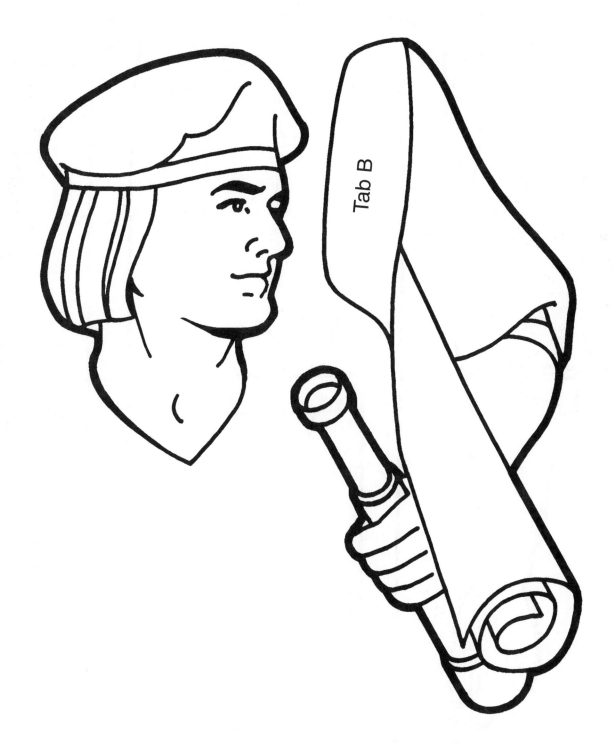

Christopher Columbus *(cont.)*

Christopher Columbus *(cont.)*

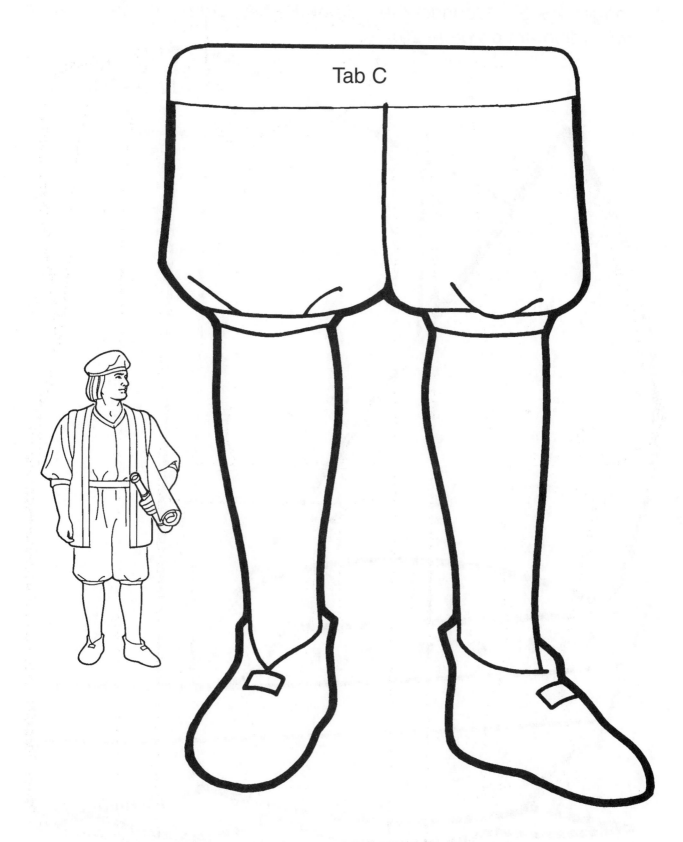

Tab C

Ship

Use pages 28–30. Connect the ship at the tab. Add sail and cross as shown in diagram on page 29.

Ship *(cont.)*

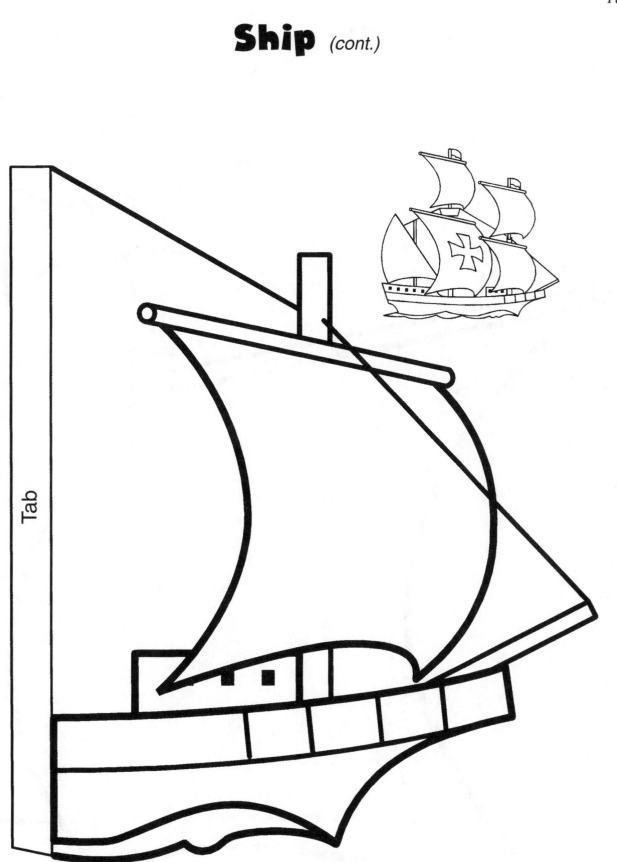

Tab

Ship *(cont.)*

30   © *Teacher Created Materials, Inc.*

Jack O'Lantern

Use pages 31–32. Connect the Jack O' Lantern at the tab.

Tab

Jack O'Lantern *(cont.)*

Spooky House

Use pages 33–34. Connect the house at the tab.

Tab

Spooky House *(cont.)*

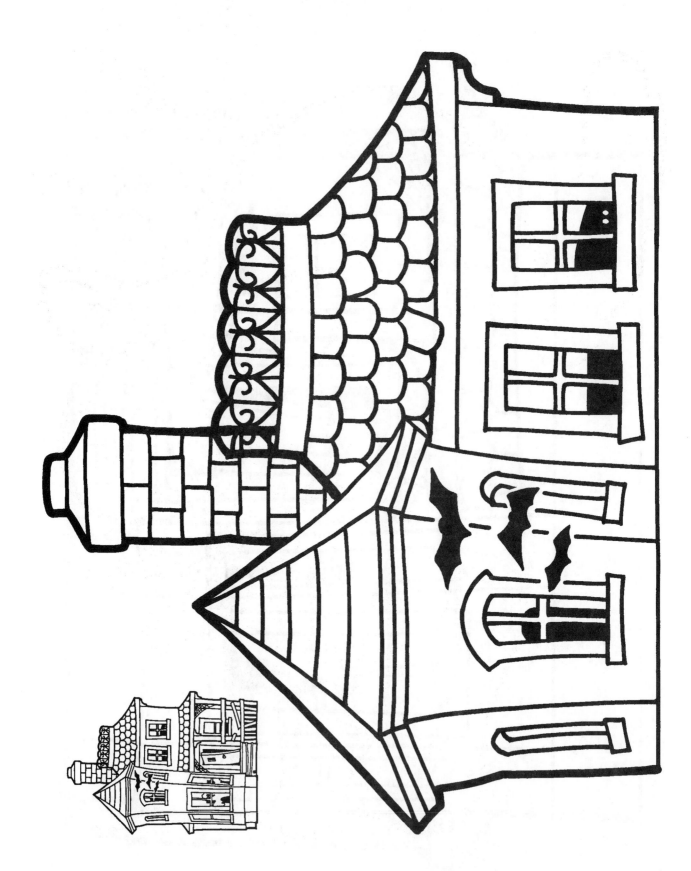

34

Cat

Bat

Skeleton

Use pages 37–39. Attach the skull to Tab A. Connect the upper and lower arms to Tabs C & D. Attach the left arm to Tab B and the right arm to Tab E. Connect the upper and lower legs to Tabs H & I. Attach the left leg to Tab F and right leg to Tab G. Use brads instead of glue or tape if you want the skeleton to move.

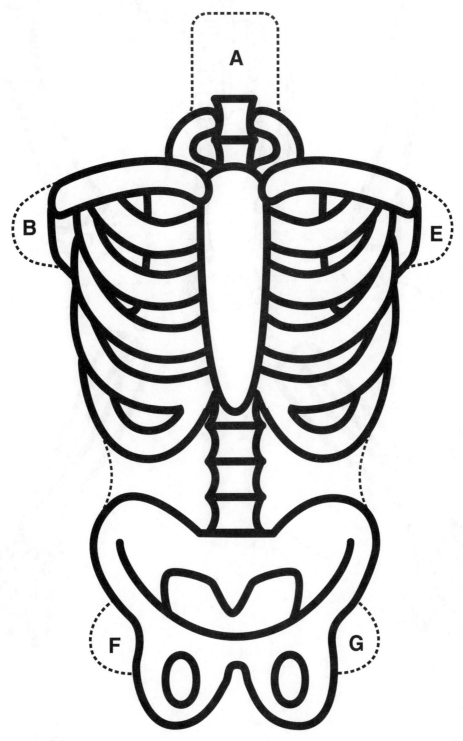

Skeleton *(cont.)*

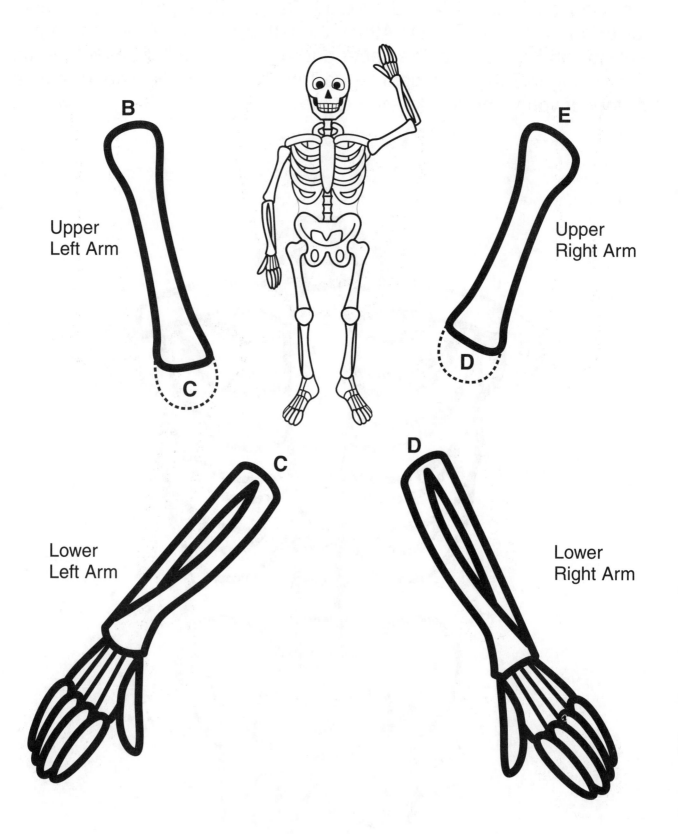

B

Upper
Left Arm

C

E

Upper
Right Arm

D

C

Lower
Left Arm

D

Lower
Right Arm

Skeleton *(cont.)*

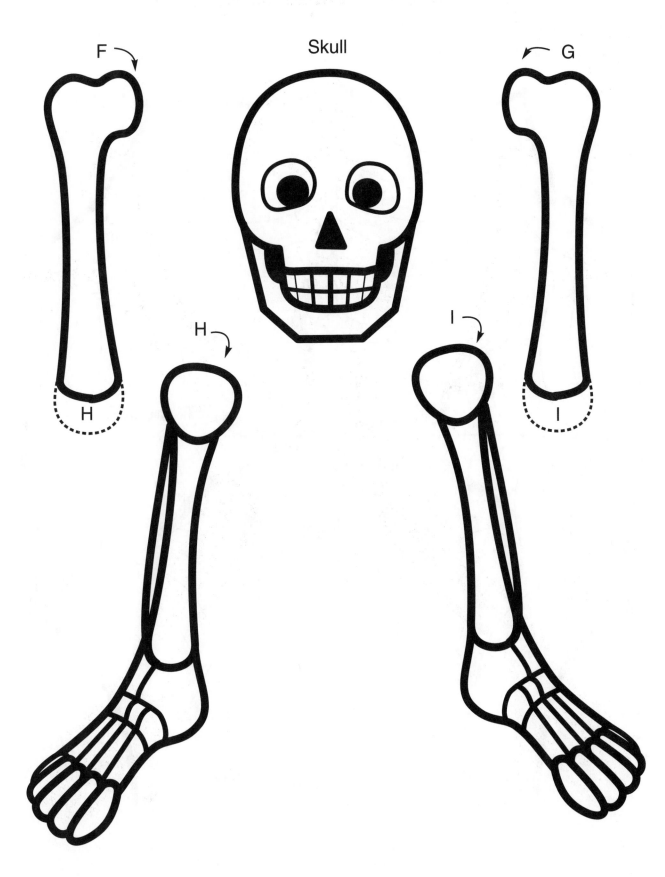

F

Skull

G

H

I

Spider and Web

Pilgrim Boy

Use pages 41–43. Attach the head to torso at Tab A. Overlap torso on legs at C and the left arm to the torso at B. This pattern was designed to work with, or without, the rifle. Determine if you wish to use the rifle. If so, do not glue the right arm down completely. Instead, attach only at shoulder at D.

Pilgrim Boy *(cont.)*

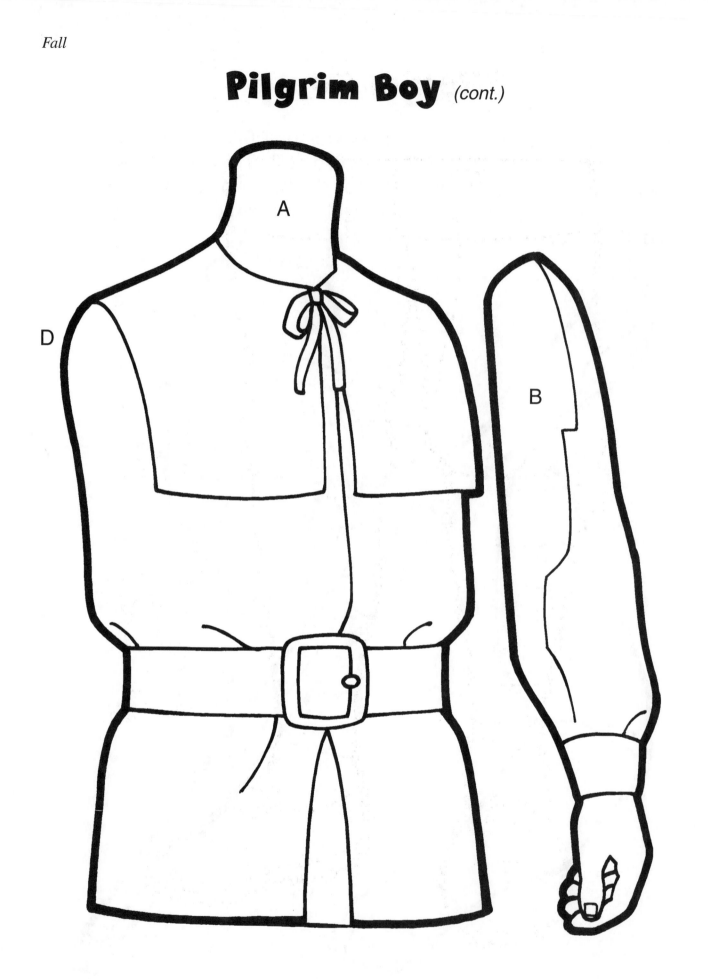

Pilgrim Boy *(cont.)*

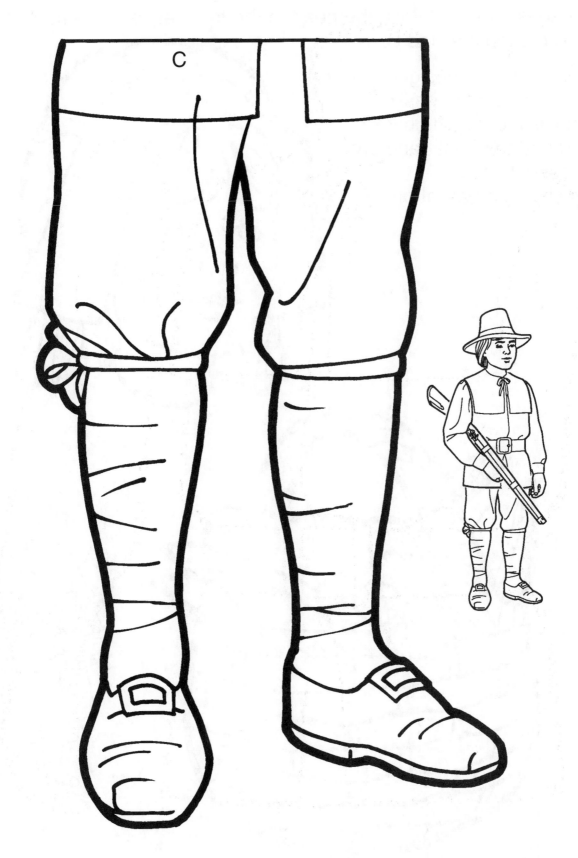

C

Pilgrim Girl

Use pages 44–46. Attach the head to the torso at Tab A. Attach the legs to the torso at Tab B.

This pattern was designed to work with, or without the basket.
If you wish to use the basket, cut around the right hand and the basket handle.
Then slide the basket on.

Pilgrim Girl *(cont.)*

A

Pilgrim Girl *(cont.)*

Tab B

46

Native American Girl

Use pages 47–49. Attach the head to torso at Tab A and legs to torso at tab B. Place vegetables in girl's left arm.

Native American Girl *(cont.)*

A

Native American Girl *(cont.)*

Tab B

Native American Boy

Use pages 50–52. Attach the head to torso at Tab A and legs to torso at Tab B. The pattern was created to make use of the bow and arrow optional. If you choose to include it, carefully cut around hand and slip bow and arrow underneath.

Native American Boy *(cont.)*

Native American Boy *(cont.)*

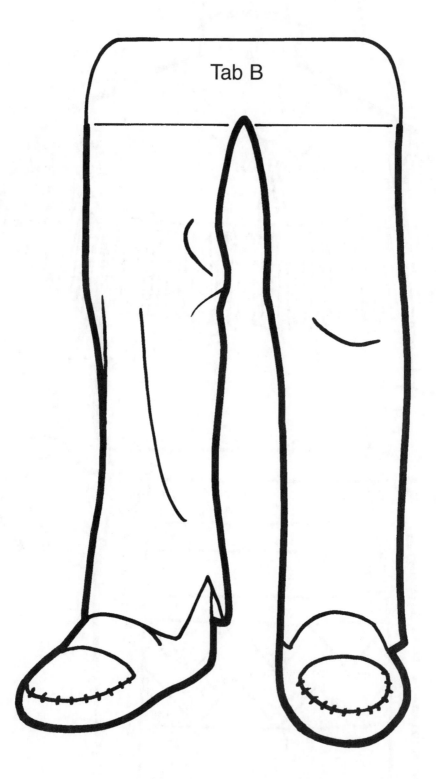

Tab B

52

Mayflower

Add this sail to the ship on pages 28–30.

Cornucopia

Use pages 54–55. Color, cut out, then glue the cornucopia together at the tab. Make a slit on the dotted line to slip in fruits and vegetables. Use reduced copies of the apple (page 21), the pumpkin (page 24), and the acorn (page 17) in addition to the vegetables and fruits (pages 56–57).

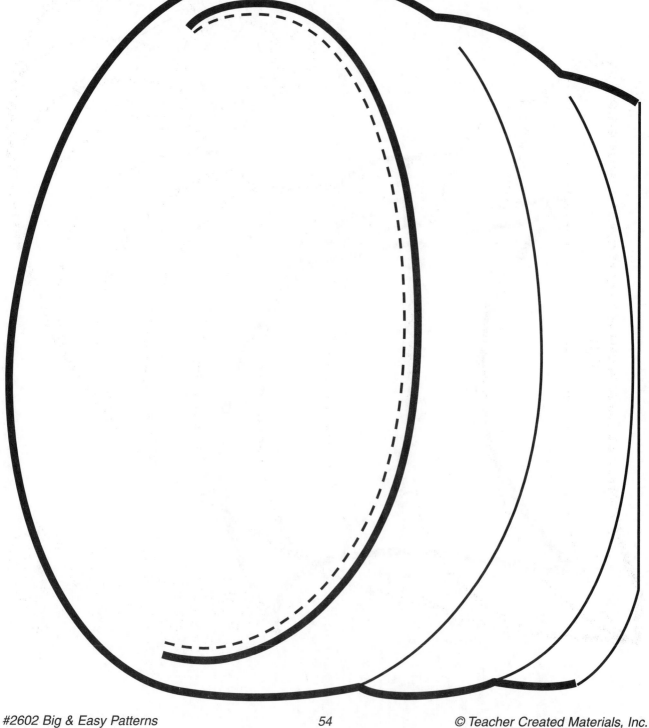

Cornucopia *(cont.)*

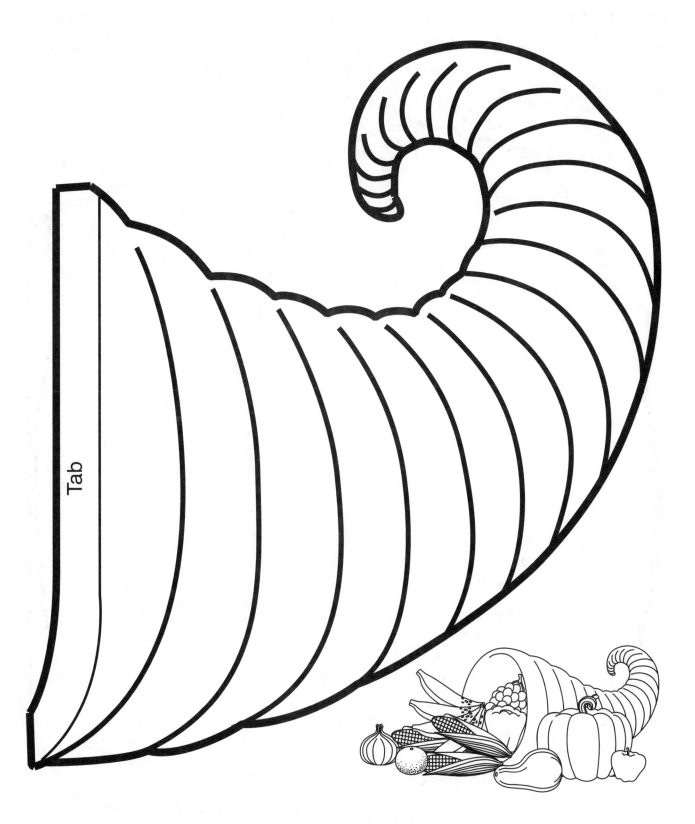

Tab

Vegetables

Fruits

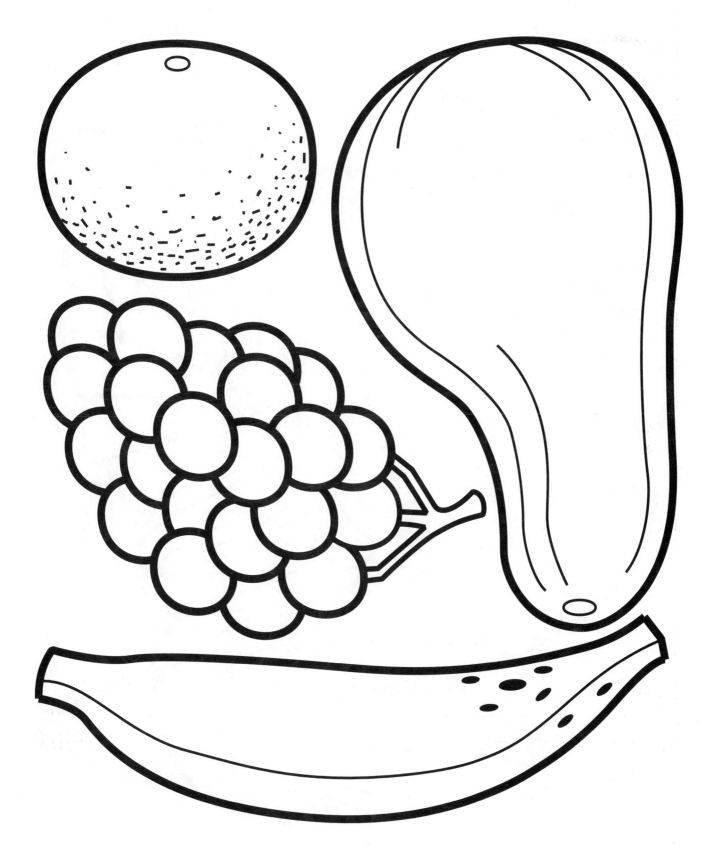

 #2602 Big & Easy Patterns

Turkey

Turkey Feathers

White out interior lines to use for word walls, math facts, etc.

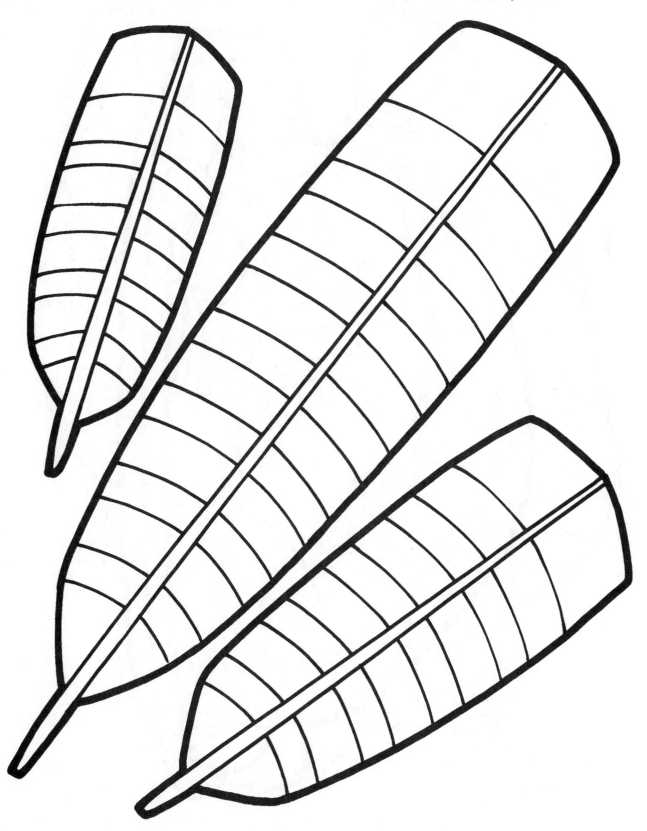

Turkey Dinner

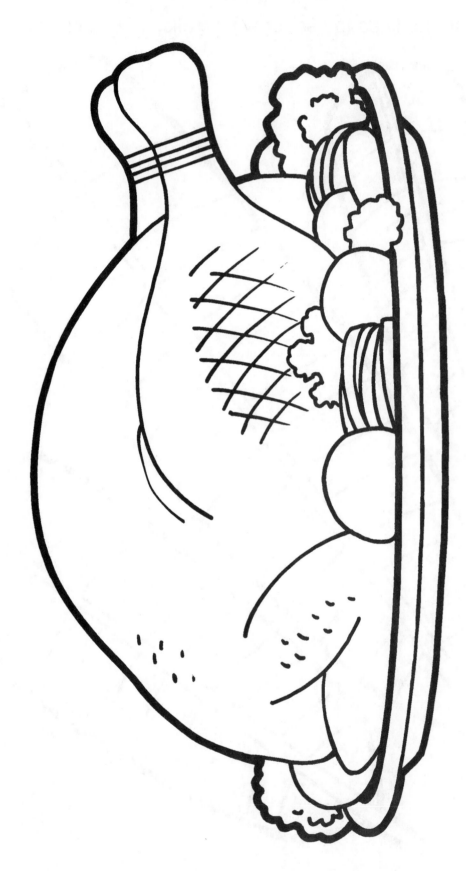

Winter Patterns and Ideas

Use the mittens and boots to create a border pattern for the bulletin board or a file folder matching game. Write questions, math facts, or letters on mittens glued to the inside of the folder. Write answers on separate mittens, and have students match the correct answer to each question.

Use the polar bear, snowman, or penguin pattern to decorate a winter bulletin board or have students create stuffed paper sculptures. Make a number matching game by gluing real buttons on the snowman and writing a numeral on each top hat. Use the egg pattern to create a penguin rookery, and write penguin facts on each egg. Use the snowflake to make a Winter Shape Book or to create a Blizzard Word Bank either on the board or hanging from the ceiling with fishing line. Decorate your room with icicles or use them as flashcards in the Math Center or as sequencing cards in the Language Arts Center.

Turn the menorahs into a number matching game. Write a number on each menorah and have the children arrange the appropriate number of candles on it. The dreidel can be stapled or laced and stuffed. The dreidel and Star of David patterns can also be used as lacing cards, shape books, bingo or tic-tac-toe cards.

Santa and the elves can be paper dolls or puppets. Create a word bank on gift patterns piled in the sleigh. Display student writing on enlarged packages around the tree or sleigh. Write spelling words on the ornaments and arrange them in alphabetical order on the Christmas tree for an interactive bulletin board. Use the stocking pattern as a shape book or as a journal cover. Run the gingerbread man on brown cardstock and lace with white yarn. Decorate the wreath with ornaments, holly, gingerbread men, and candy canes. Reduce or enlarge patterns to fit.

Use the mkeka (placemat) for a real classroom feast or as part of your Kwanzaa bulletin board. Use the potato pattern as well as apples, oranges, bananas, and grapes to create a Kwanzaa Word Bank. The kikombe (cup) pattern can be used to create a big book about Kwanzaa. Use the pattern of Dr. Martin Luther King, Jr. as a puppet, a story prompt, or an art project. Color the rainbow with a variety of skin tone colors and display on the bulletin board. Display student writing on clouds around the rainbow.

The valentine heart pattern can be used as a bingo card, lacing card, shape book, or for a sorting or patterning game. Use the mailbox for a word bank with hearts of different colors spilling out of it. Arrange the groundhog, flashlight, and shadow patterns on the board to explain how shadows are made. Make a file folder matching game with groundhogs and black circles for groundhog holes. Use Lincoln's log cabin for a shape book about Lincoln or a word bank for president words. Color and cut the cherry tree and decorate with cinnamon candies. Write a rule such as "Tell the truth." on the hatchet.

Write words on gold coins to make a St. Patrick's Day Word Bank or make a number matching game by writing a numeral on each pot and placing the appropriate number of coins on it. Use the shamrock pattern as a lacing card or a shape book. Have students create leprechaun faces on paper plates and attach the ears and yarn for hair, or make head bands, sized to fit around students' heads, and glue on the pointed ears.

Jacket

Suggest that students draw themselves in the head opening of the jacket or cut out the circle and replace with pictures of students.

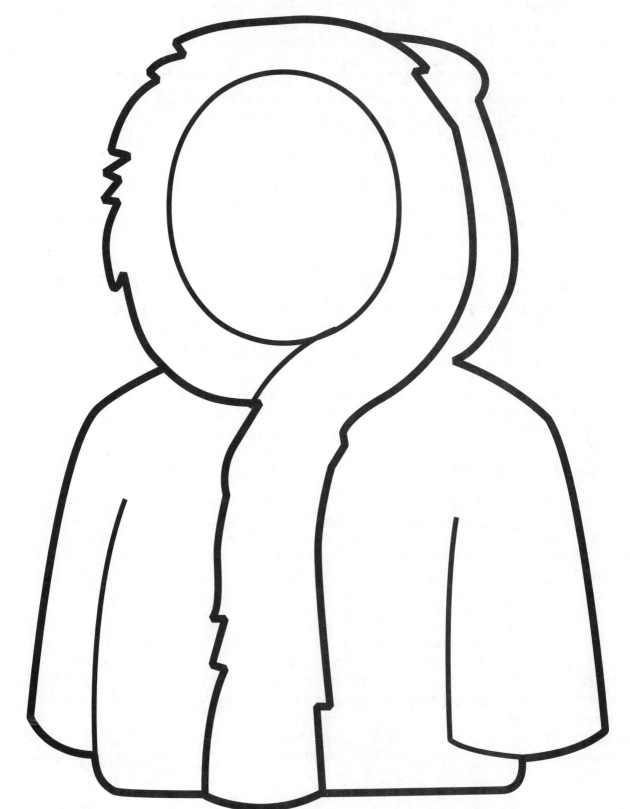

Cap & Boots

The cap and boots can be used with the snowman on page 68.

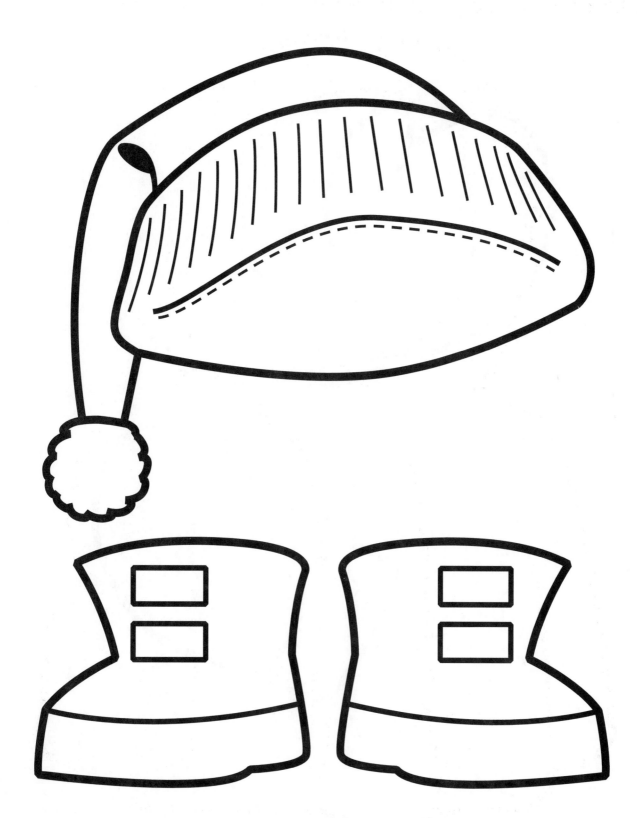

Mittens

Mittens can be used to create borders, word walls, etc. Try them on the snowman on page 68.

Polar Bear

Use pages 65–67. Attach the polar bear's head to the torso at Tab A.
Attach the legs B, C, D, and E as marked. Attach the tail at Tab F.

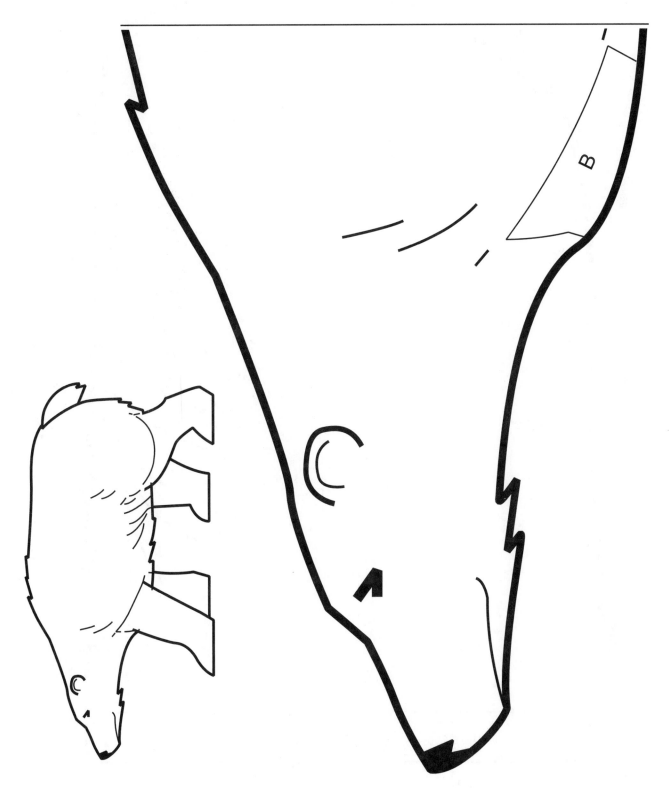

Polar Bear *(cont.)*

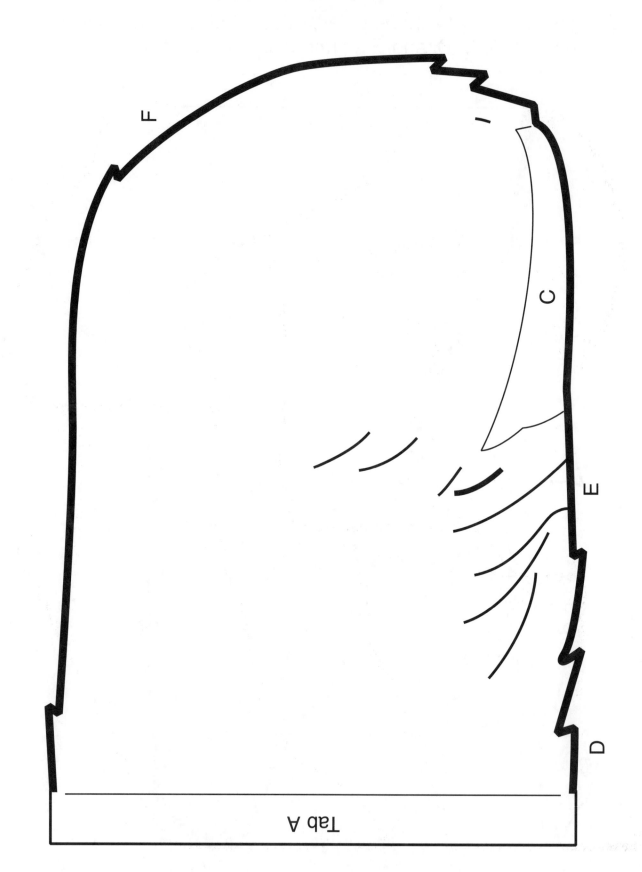

Polar Bear *(cont.)*

Snowman

Use pages 68–69. Try the snow cap on page 63 to decorate your snowman. You may also wish to use mittens (page 64) and boots (page 63) to dress your snowman. Attach the snowman head to the tab. Place branch arms where appropriate.

Snowman *(cont.)*

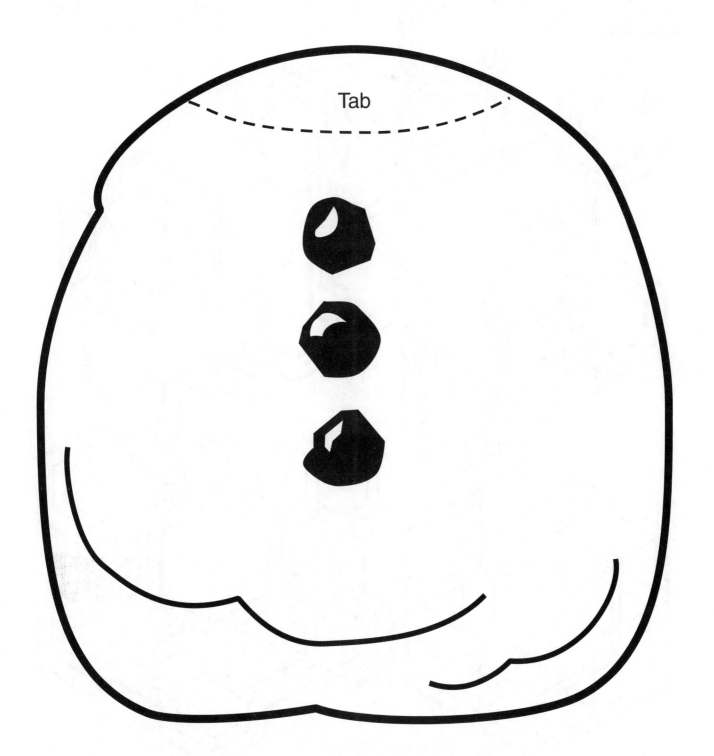

Tab

Snowflakes

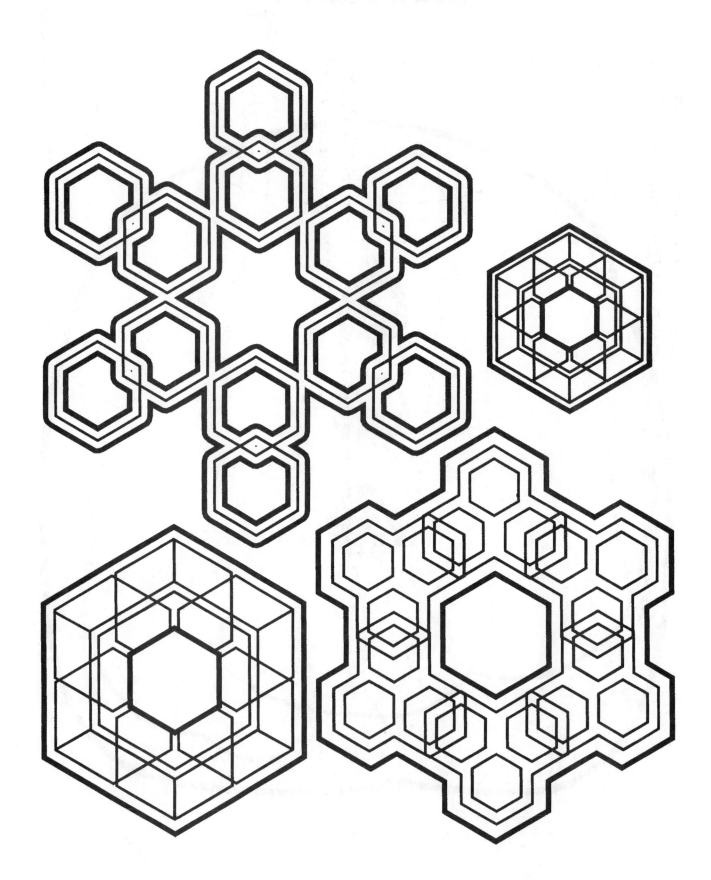

Icicles

Penguin

Use pages 72–74. Overlap torso on tab A. Attach the wings at B & C.
Attach the feet at D & E.

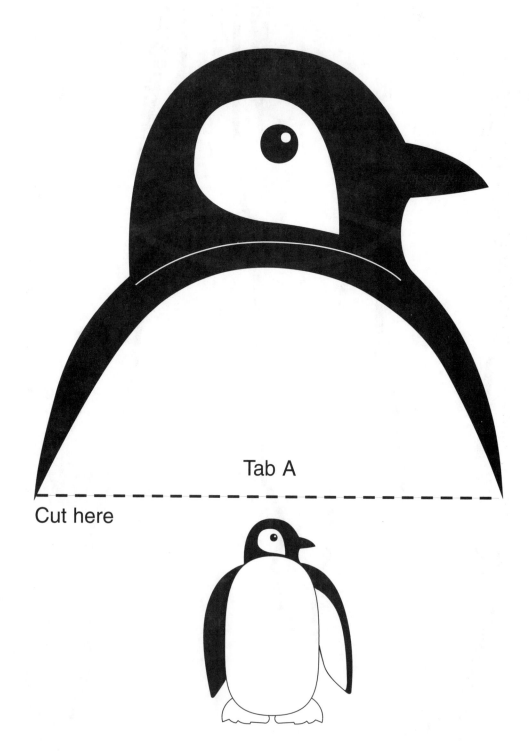

Tab A

Cut here

Penguin *(cont.)*

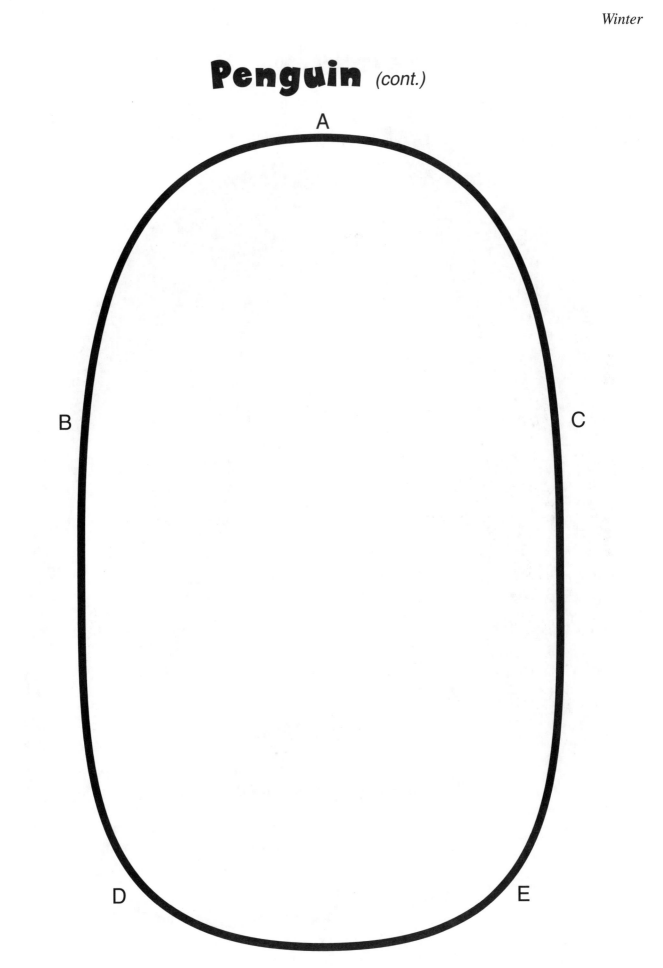

Penguin *(cont.)*

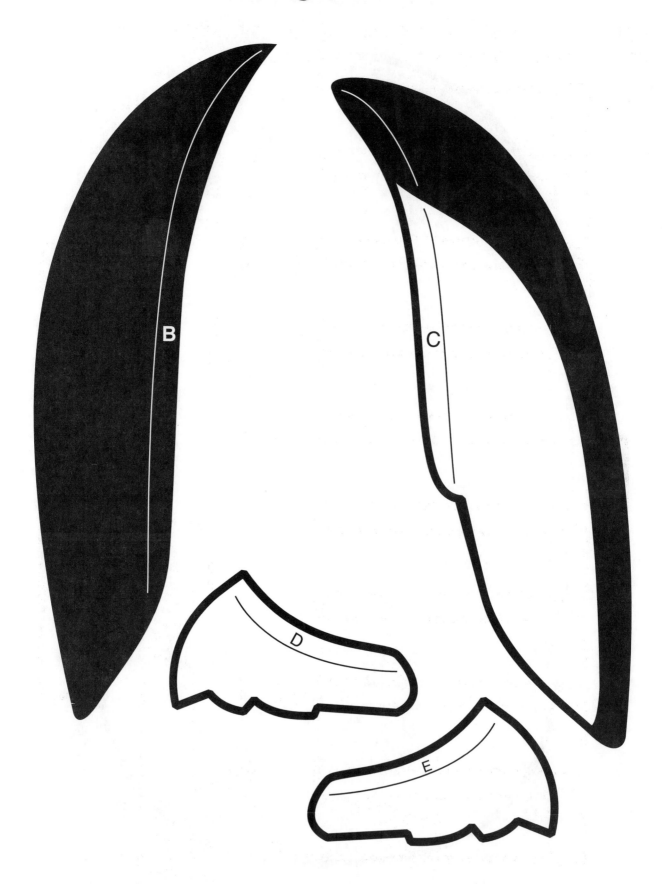

74

Menorah

Duplicate candle shown or make your own with strips of construction paper or wrapping paper.

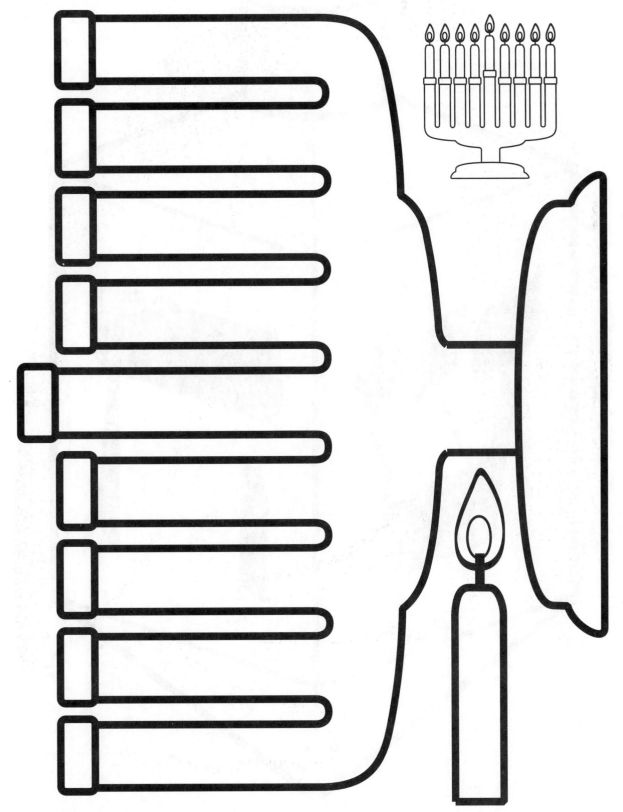

Dreidel

76

Dreidel *(cont.)*

77

Star of David

Santa Claus

Use pages 79–81. Overlap torso on pants at Tab A. Place bag of gifts below left mitten.

Santa Claus *(cont.)*

Tab A

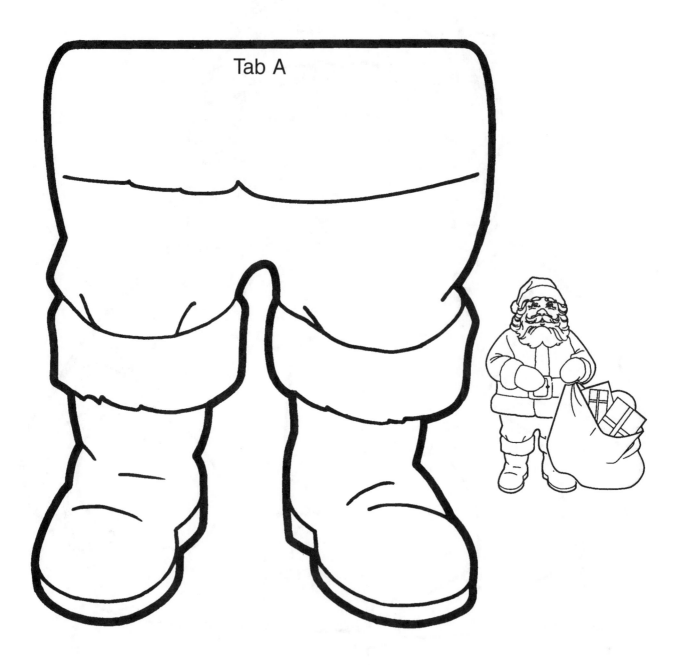

Santa Claus *(cont.)*

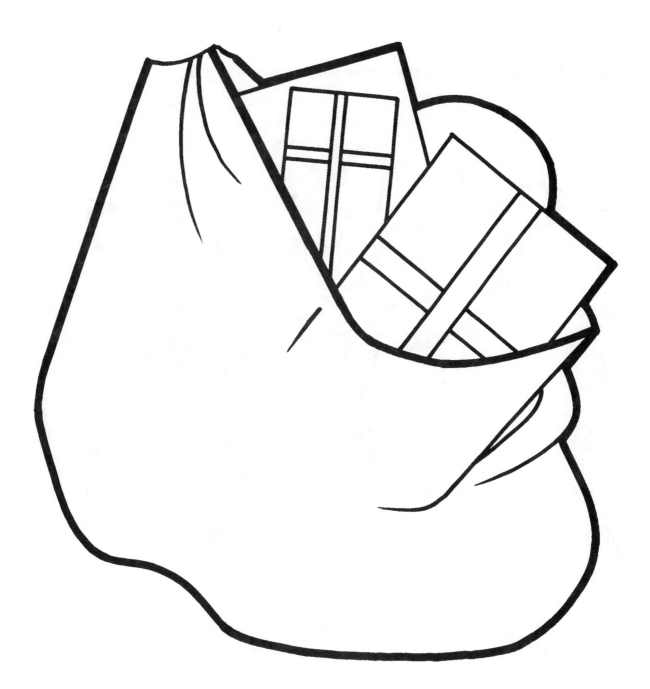

Reindeer

Use pages 82–84. Attach the reindeer's head to the torso at Tab A.
Connect the torso at Tab B.

A

Reindeer *(cont.)*

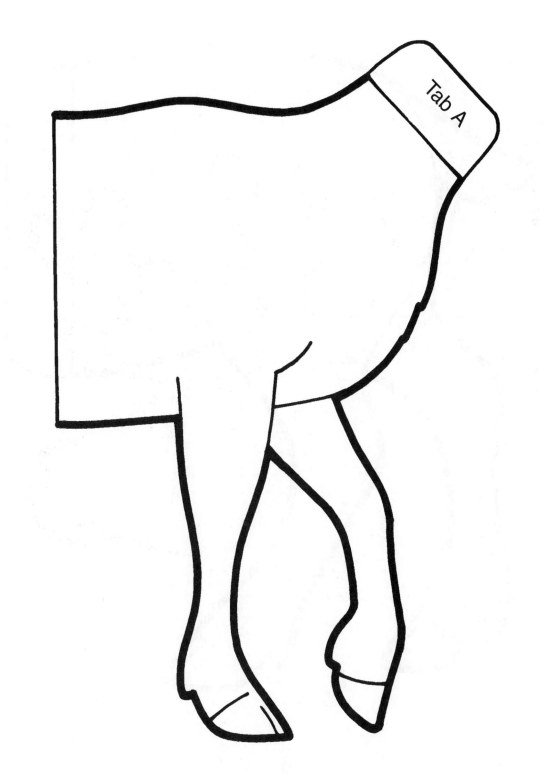

Tab A

Reindeer *(cont.)*

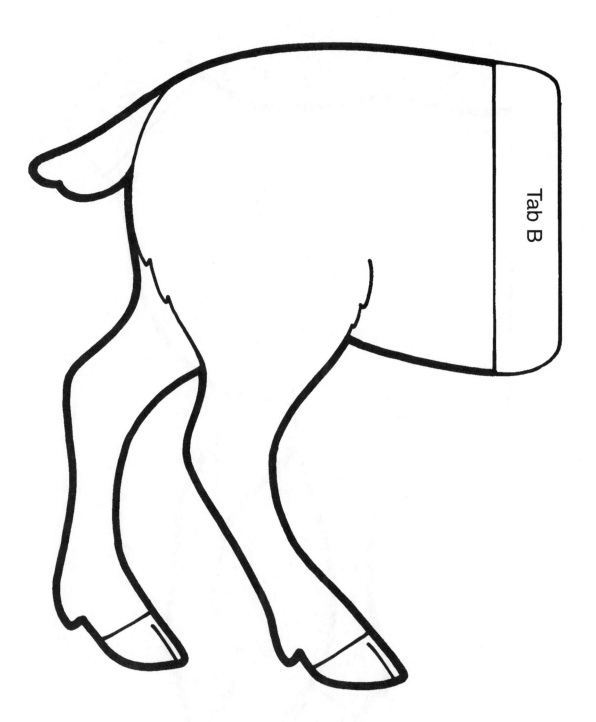

Tab B

Elf

Sitting Elf

The sitting elf was created to sit in the sleigh on pages 87–88.

Sleigh

Use pages 87–88. Connect the sleigh at the tab. Use with Santa, elves and reindeer on preceding pages.

Sleigh *(cont.)*

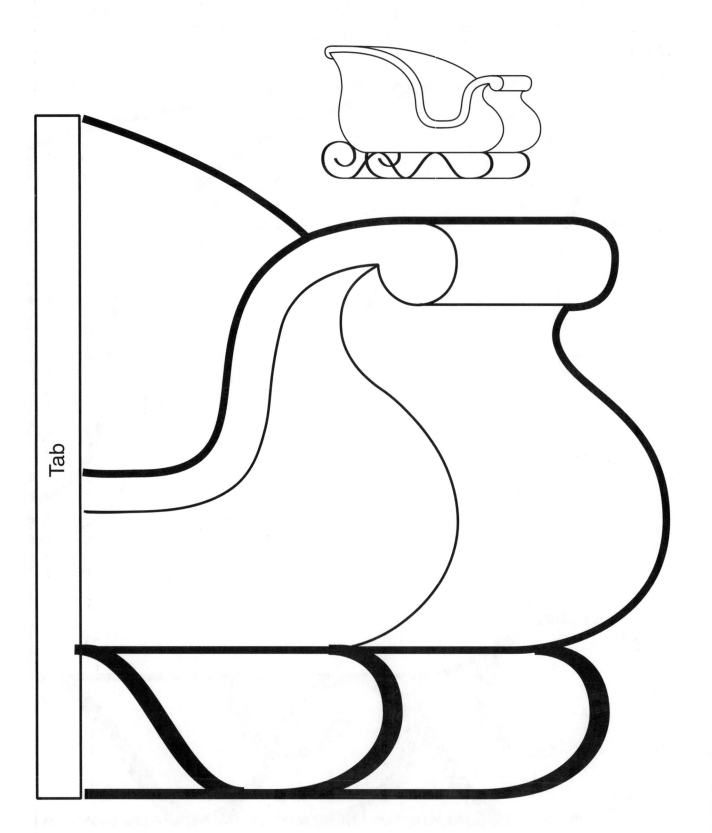

Tab

Christmas Tree

Use pages 89–91. Attach the top of tree to midsection at Tab A. Attach the midsection to base at Tab B. Place star on the top of the tree and decorate.

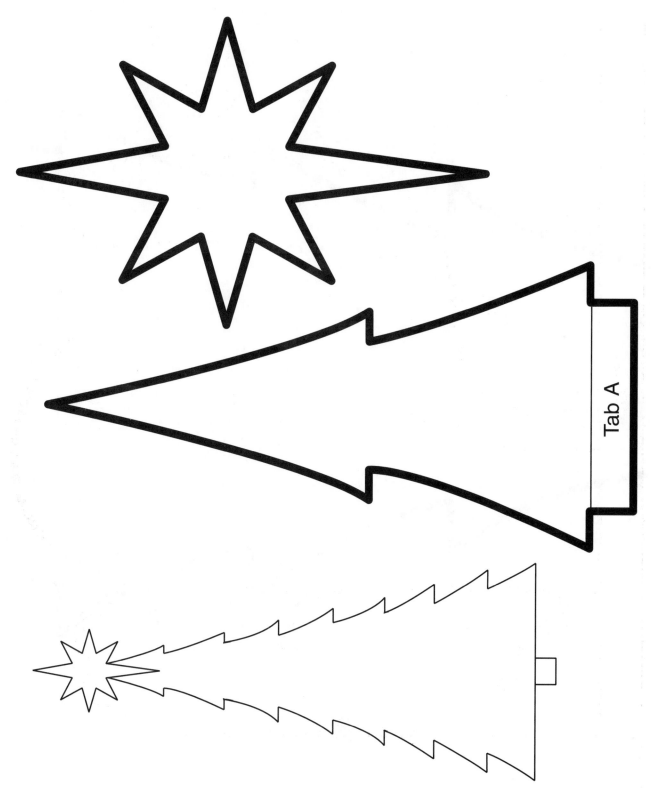

Christmas Tree *(cont.)*

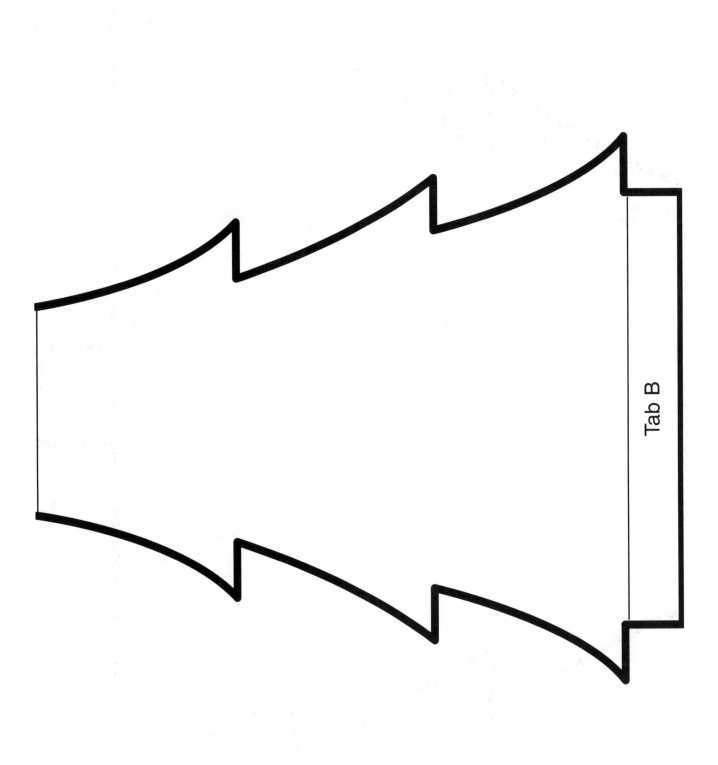

Tab B

Christmas Tree *(cont.)*

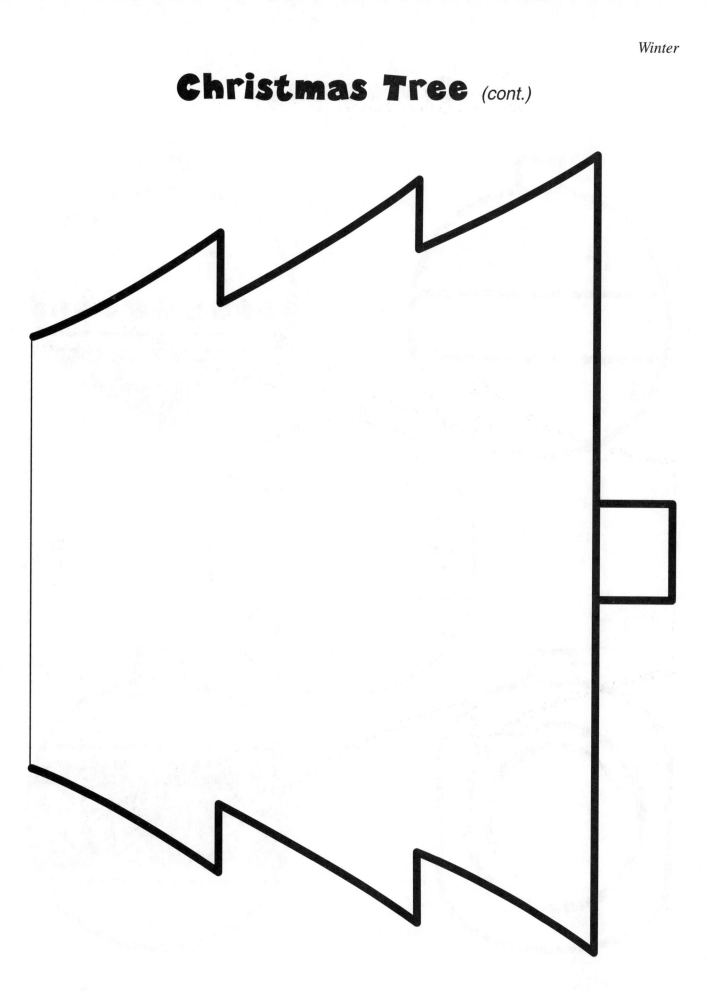

Ornaments

Gift

Stocking

Gingerbread Man

Use pages 95–96. Attach the arms and legs to the back of the torso.

Arm   Arm

Leg   Leg

Gingerbread Man *(cont.)*

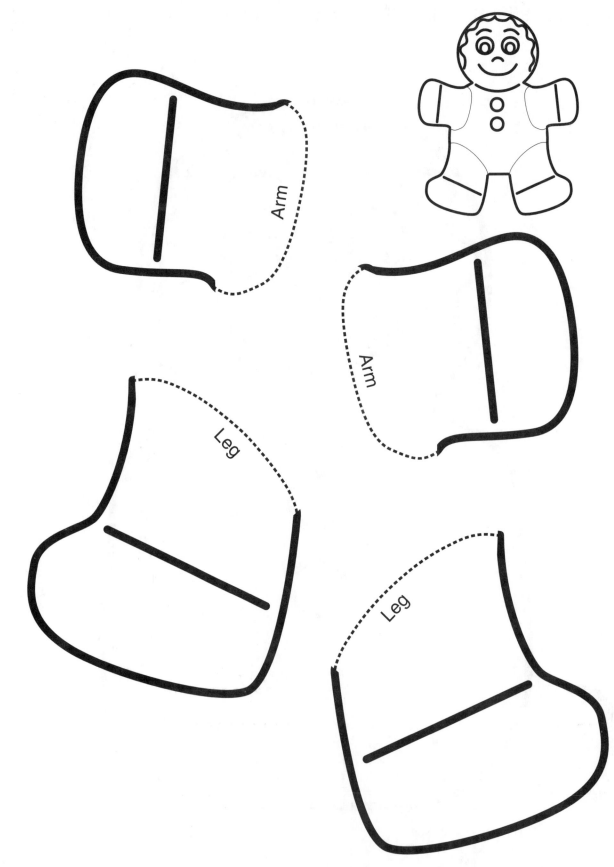

96

Candy Cane

Use pages 97–98. Connect the candy cane at the tab.

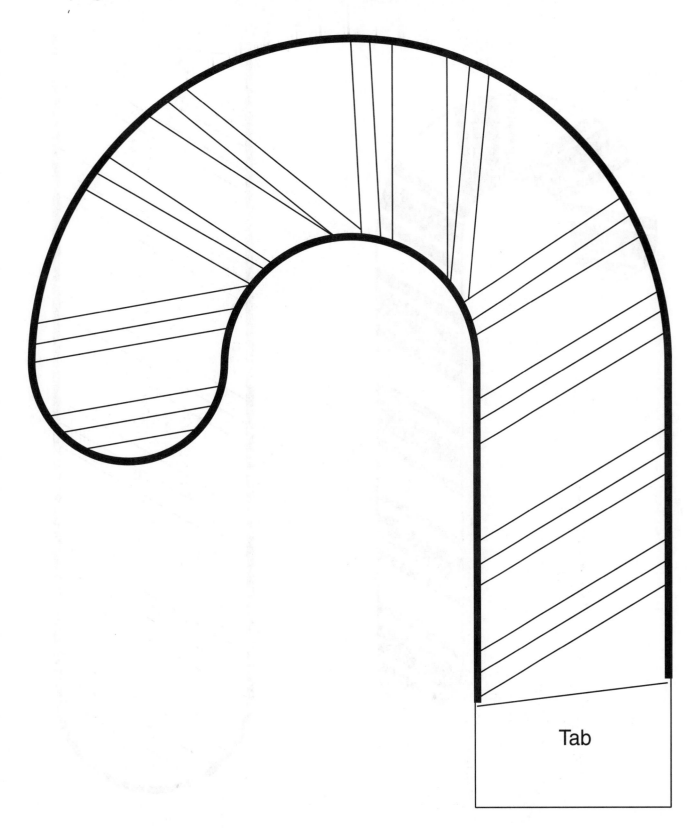

Tab

Candy Cane *(cont.)*

98

Wreath

Use pages 99–100. Connect the wreath at tabs.

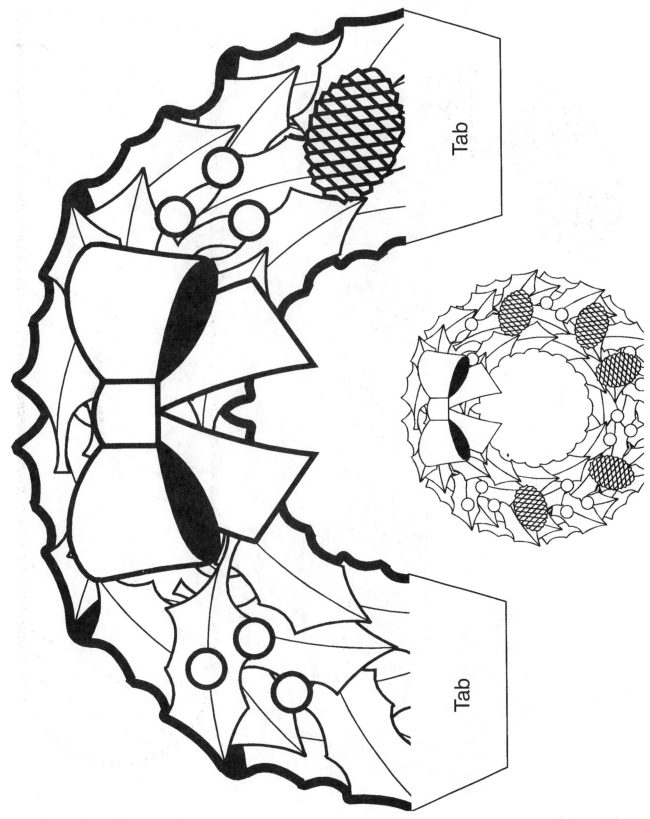

Wreath *(cont.)*

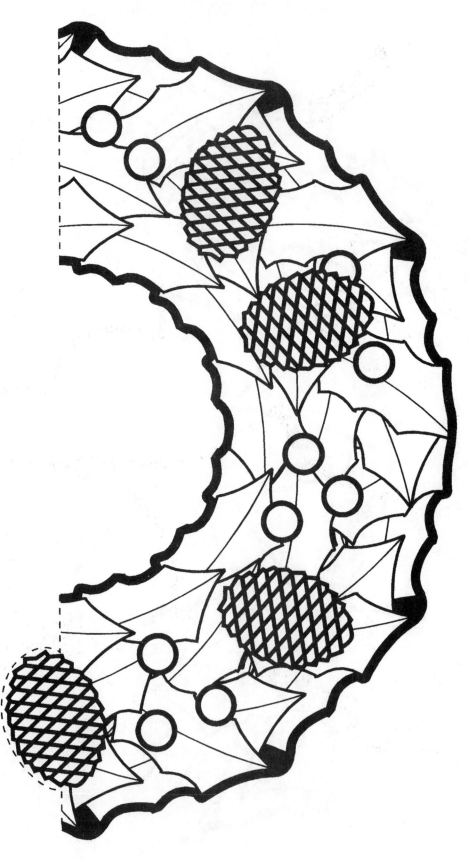

Holly

Mistletoe

102

Kinara

The kinara is a special candleholder with seven candles used during Kwanzaa. Three candles should be red and three should be green. The central candle is black.

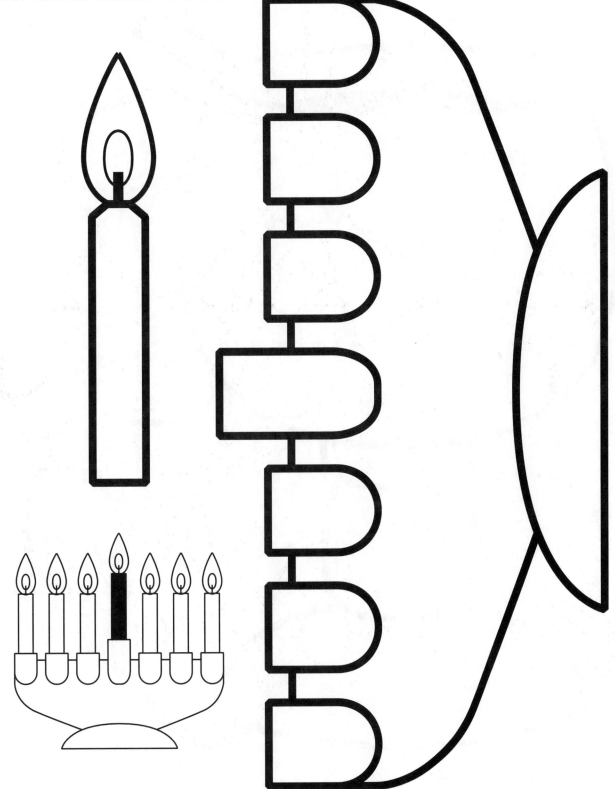

Kikombe

Use the kikombe (cup) in a Kwanzaa display and surround it with fruits (pages 21 & 57) and vegetables (page 56).

Mkeka

The mkeka is the first symbol of Kwanzaa. Traditionally, the mkeka is woven into interesting patterns. Have students create their own designs using crayons or markers.

New Year's Party Hat

106

Martin Luther King, Jr.

Use pages 107–109. Attach the head to torso at Tab A. Connect the
left arm to torso at Tab B and legs to torso at Tab C.

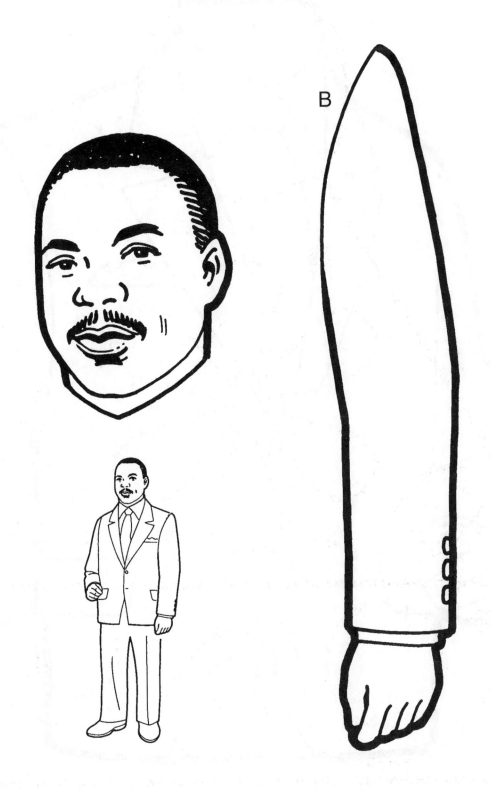

Martin Luther King, Jr. *(cont.)*

Martin Luther King, Jr. *(cont.)*

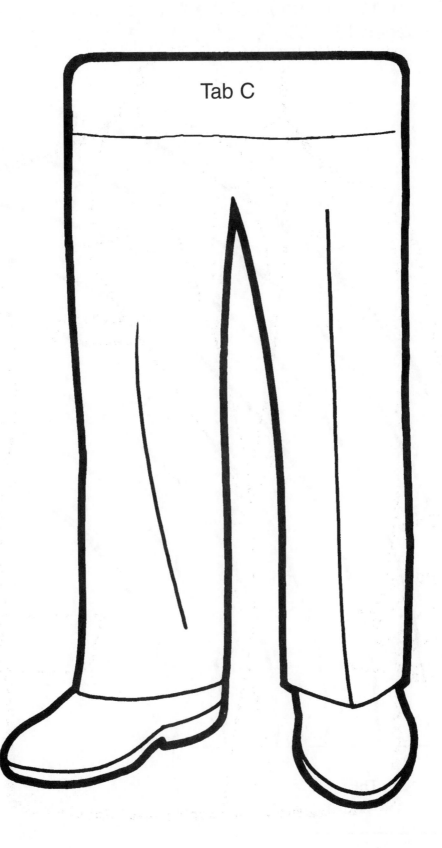

Tab C

Rainbow

Use pages 110–111. Connect at the tab. You may wish to add the clouds from pages 167–168.

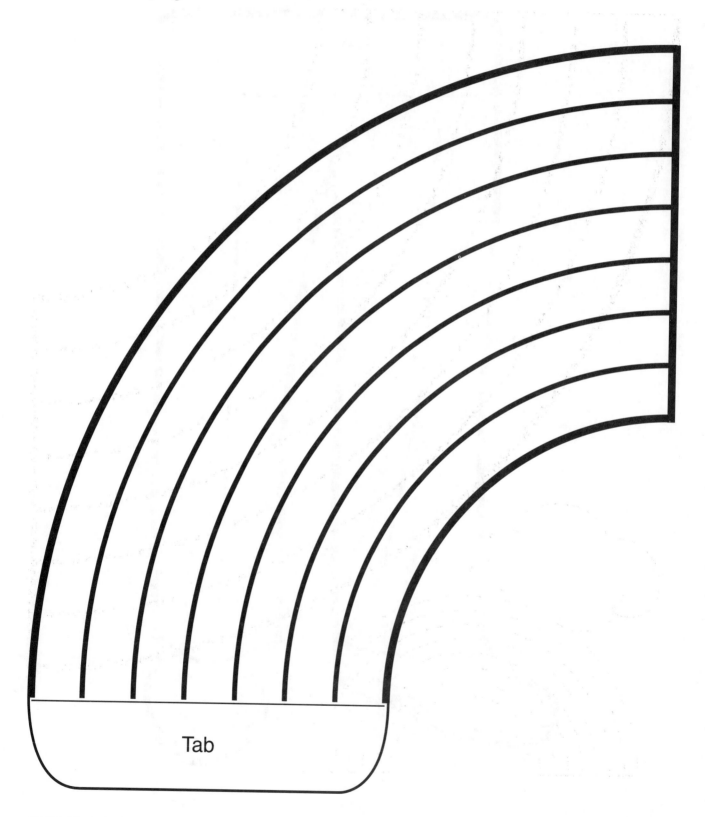

Tab

Rainbow *(cont.)*

Groundhog

Use with page 113.

Groundhog Shadow and Flashlight

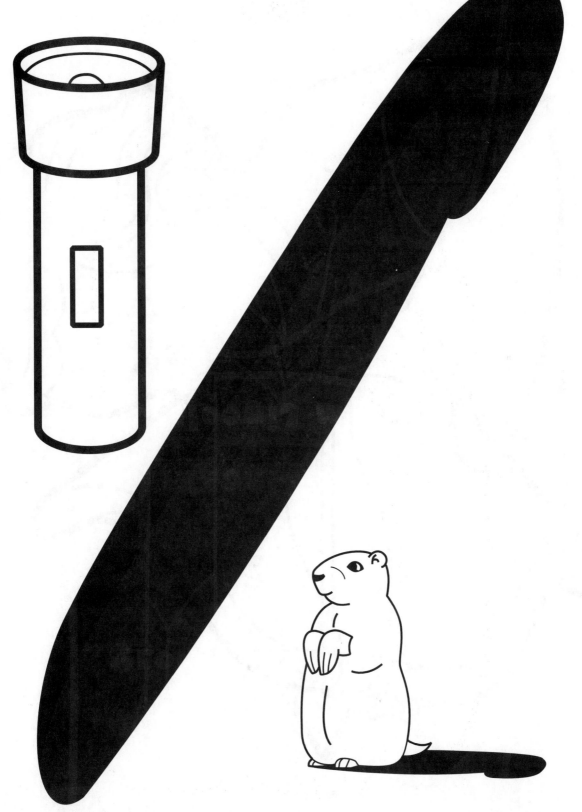

Cupid

Use pages 114–115. Connect the Cupid at Tab A.
Add the wings at Tab B.

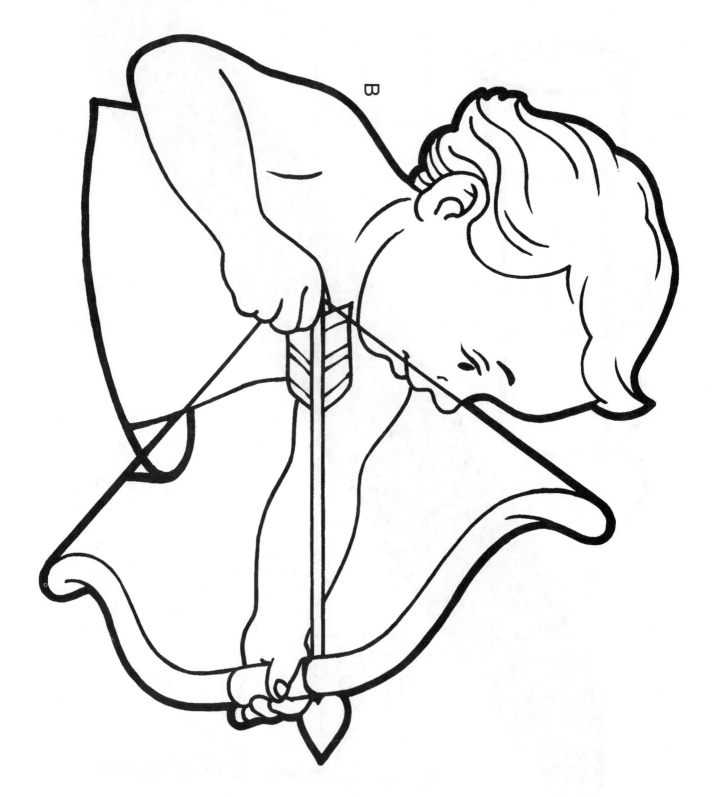

Cupid *(cont.)*

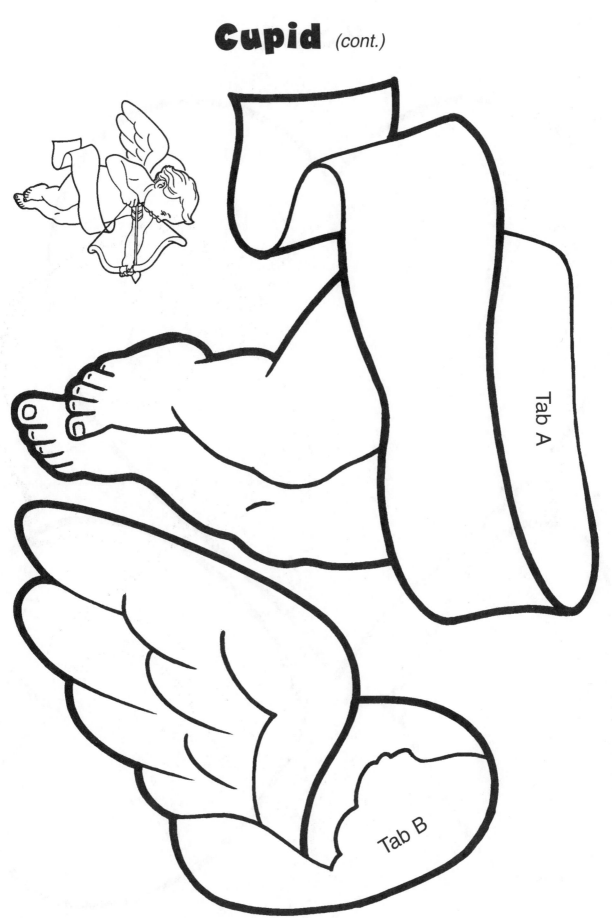

Tab A

Tab B

Hearts

Valentine Heart

Mailbox

Use pages 118–119. Connect the mailbox at the tab. Place flag in the desired position. Cut a strip of poster board if you want your mailbox to have a post.

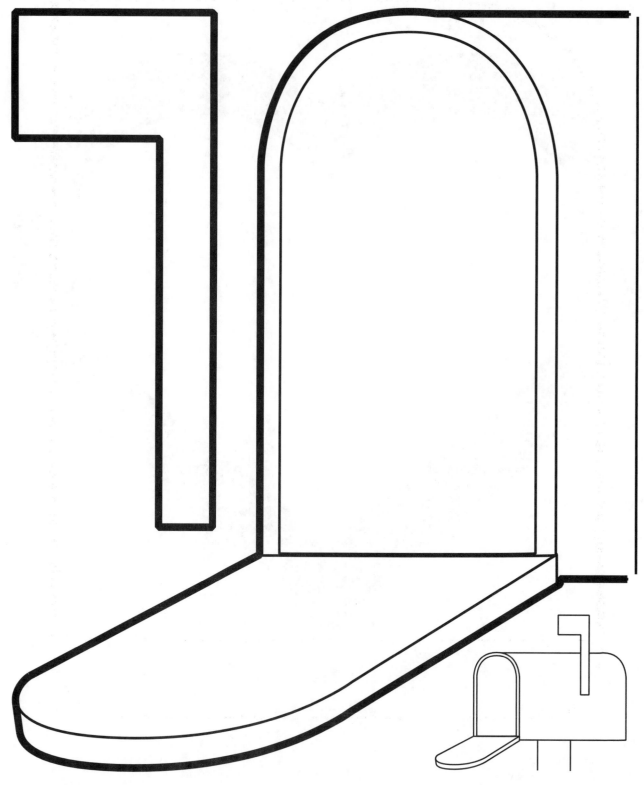

Mailbox *(cont.)*

Tab

Envelope

Use pages 120–121. Fold down the three flaps. (See diagram.) Apply a small amount of glue to the flaps and press on the other envelope piece. When dry, place a valentine inside, and seal with a sticker.

Place glue here on flap.

Place glue here on flap.

Place glue here on flap.

Envelope *(cont.)*

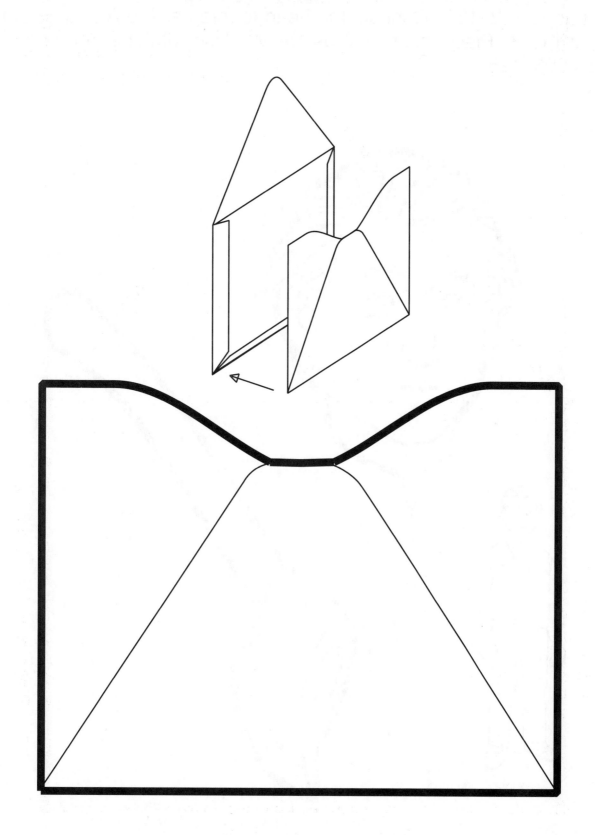

George Washington

Use pages 122–124. Connect the head to torso at Tab A and torso to legs at Tab B. Place ax in hand as shown. Use with cherry tree on pages 125–126.

George Washington *(cont.)*

Tab A

George Washington *(cont.)*

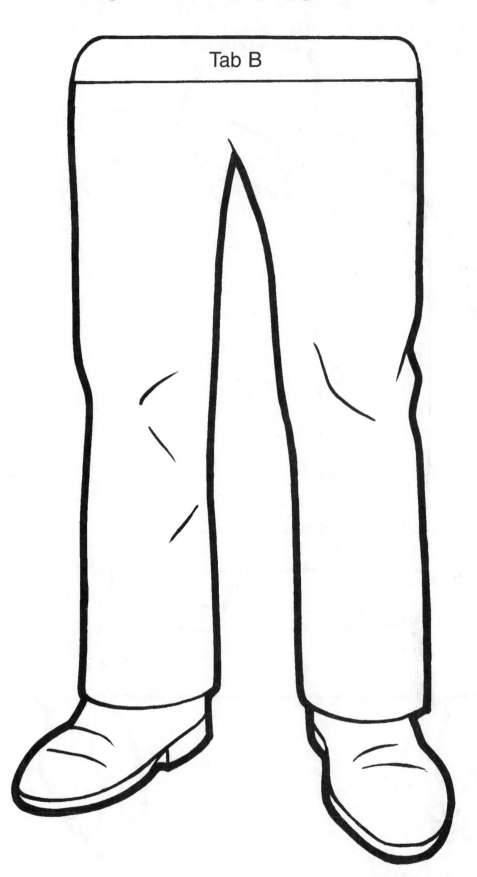

Tab B

124

Cherry Tree

Use pages 125–126. Overlap tree trunk at Tab A. Color and add cherries.

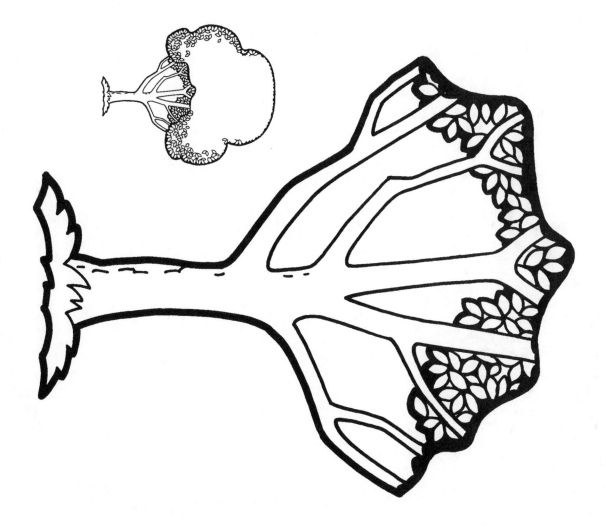

Cherry Tree *(cont.)*

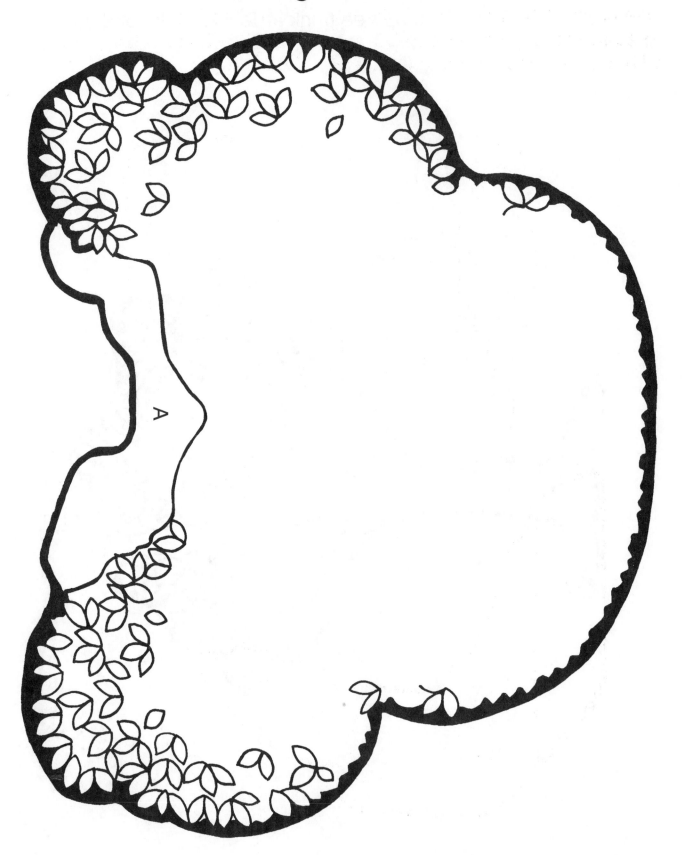

Abraham Lincoln

Use pages 127–129. Attach the head to torso at Tab A and legs to torso at Tab B. The left arm is attached to the torso at Tab C. Use with the log cabin on pages 130–131.

Abraham Lincoln *(cont.)*

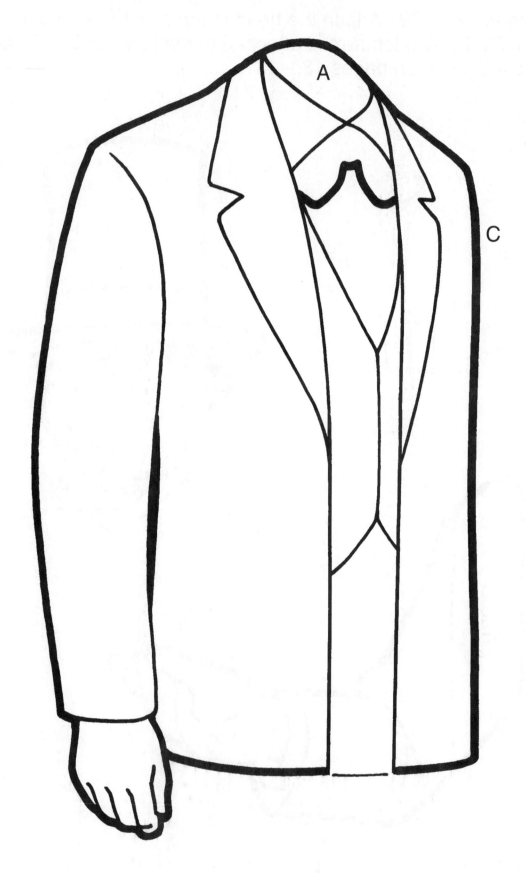

Abraham Lincoln *(cont.)*

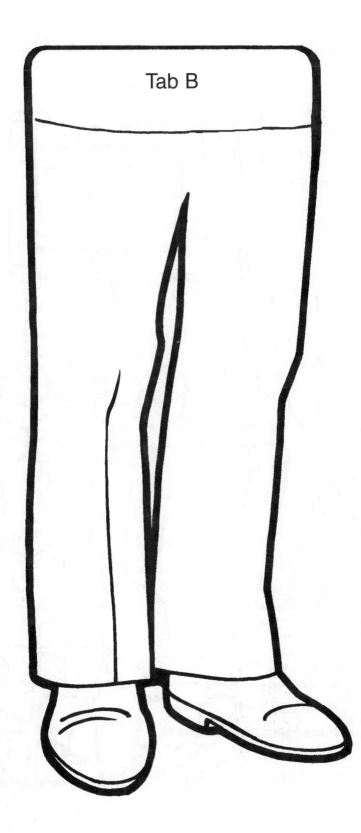

Tab B

Log Cabin

Use pages 130–131. Connect the cabin at the tab.

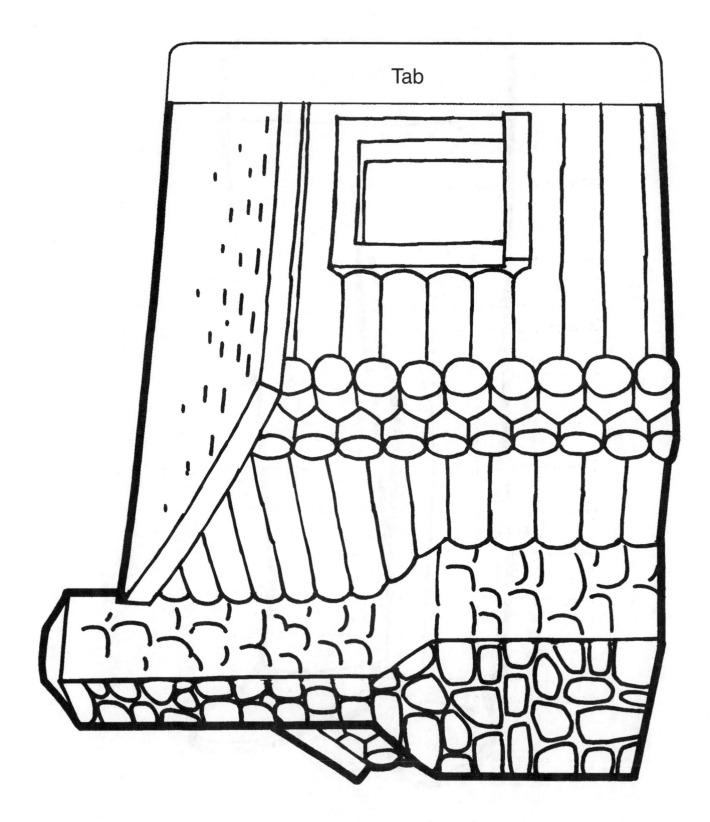

Tab

Log Cabin *(cont.)*

Leprechaun

Use pages 132–133. Overlap torso at the tab. Attach the walking stick to the left hand.

Leprechaun *(cont.)*

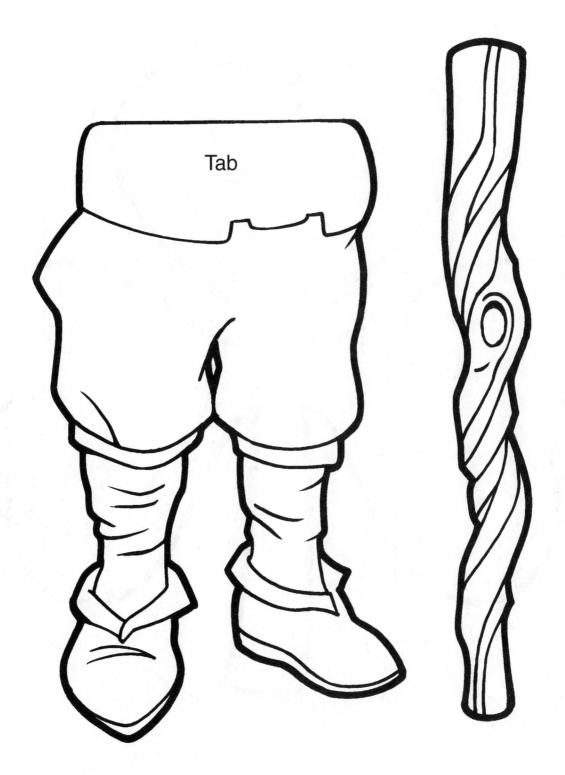

Tab

Shamrock

Pot of Gold

Use with rainbow (pages 110–111) and clouds (pages 167–168).

Leprechaun Ears and Gold Coin

Fold tabs on ears and attach to a headband or a paper plate.

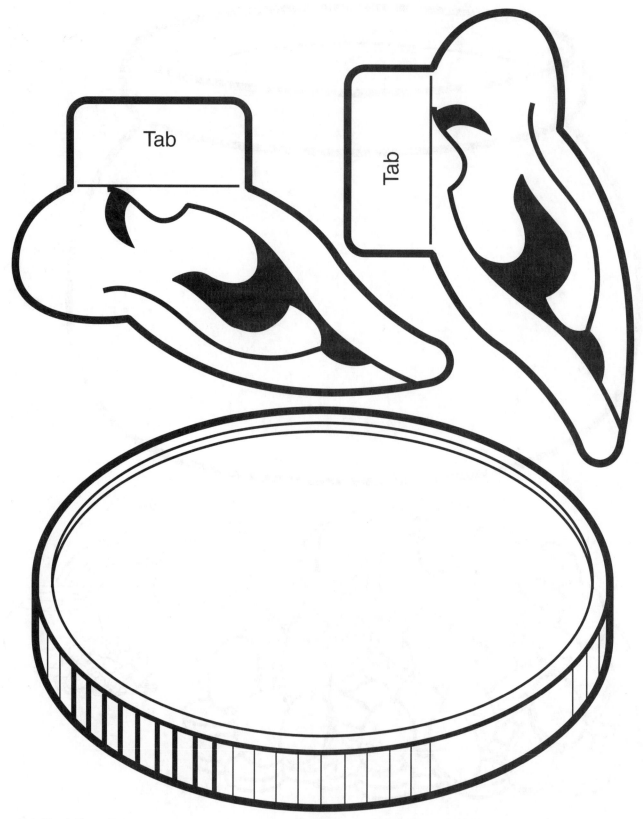

Spring Patterns and Ideas

Create matching games for consonant sounds, rhyming words, or upper and lowercase letters using the beehive and bees, nest and eggs, or cracked eggs and chicks. Clip bees to the hive with clothespins.

The seed packet pattern can be enlarged and used as a big book, a math work mat, or reduced and used to label a flower or vegetable graph. Staple or lace two flower pot patterns together and insert daffodils, tulips, and a seed packet on a craft stick. Pots can also be used for bingo or tic-tac-toe games.

Write a worm poem as a class, and record the poem in an Inchworm Shape Book. Use the small inchworm to measure items in the class. Glue 12 inchworms to a strip of tagboard to make an inchworm ruler. The small inchworm pattern is one inch long; the large inchworm pattern is 12 inches long.

The farm animal patterns can be used as puppets, story props, or in your Drama Center. Create a farmyard story and record it in a Barn Big Book. Sort pictures of animals from magazines into Animals Who Live in Barns and Animals Who Don't Live in Barns.

Attach a long length of yarn to the end of the kite pattern, write words on the tail, and attach them to the yarn for a word bank. Make an interactive bulletin board by punching a hole at the bottom of the kite and tying on a thick piece of yarn. Print a concept you are teaching on each kite and answers on the tails. Glue a small piece of Velcro to the back of each tail and match tails to the correct kite. Make a cloud pillow tracing an enlarged cloud pattern onto two pieces of butcher paper, cutting it out, stapling it, and stuffing it. Hang silver tinsel or blue crepe paper streamers from the bottom of the cloud.

The raindrop pattern can be a shape book, bingo or lacing card, or printed in several sizes and used as a sorting or patterning activity. Make a raindrop mobile by suspending raindrops from the umbrella pattern. Create a word bank with the umbrella and the raindrops, or show off student weather poetry by mounting poems on raindrops or clouds.

Small bunnies can be used as math manipulatives, puppets, or paper dolls. Reduce the Easter egg pattern and have students make pattern placemats with eggs, bunnies, and carrots. Have students create bunny faces on paper plates or make headbands and attach the bunny ears. Use the basket and egg patterns to collect Easter words. Stitch two basket patterns together, insert a large Easter egg pattern and plastic Easter grass.

Use the I Love You, Mom, or Dad patterns to make cards to hold original poems or sentiments. The rose pattern can be used to decorate the cards or as part of a Mother's Day bouquet along with poppies, daffodils, and tulips. Arrange flowers in the flower pot pattern and attach the bow pattern. Punch two holes at the top of the tie pattern, decorate it, and thread it with yarn to make a tie for dad.

Create Memorial Day bouquets with the poppy and bow patterns. Make a wreath by cutting out the center of a paper plate and gluing flower heads around the edge. Place a yellow bow at the bottom of the wreath, and punch a hole at the top to tie a yellow yarn loop.

Cracked Egg

Pages 138–139 form a whole egg and can be used with the chick on page 140. Cut the bottom half of the egg on the dotted line to slip in the chick.

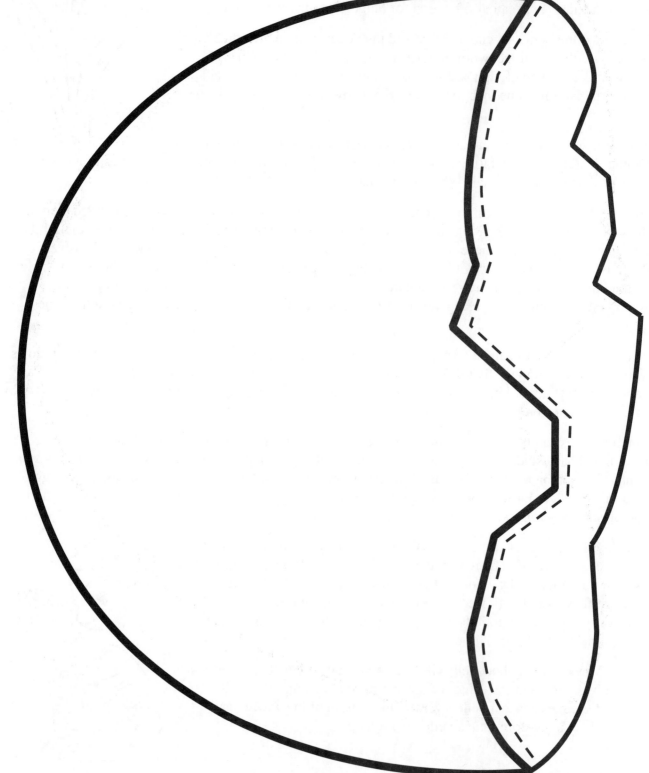

138

Cracked Egg *(cont.)*

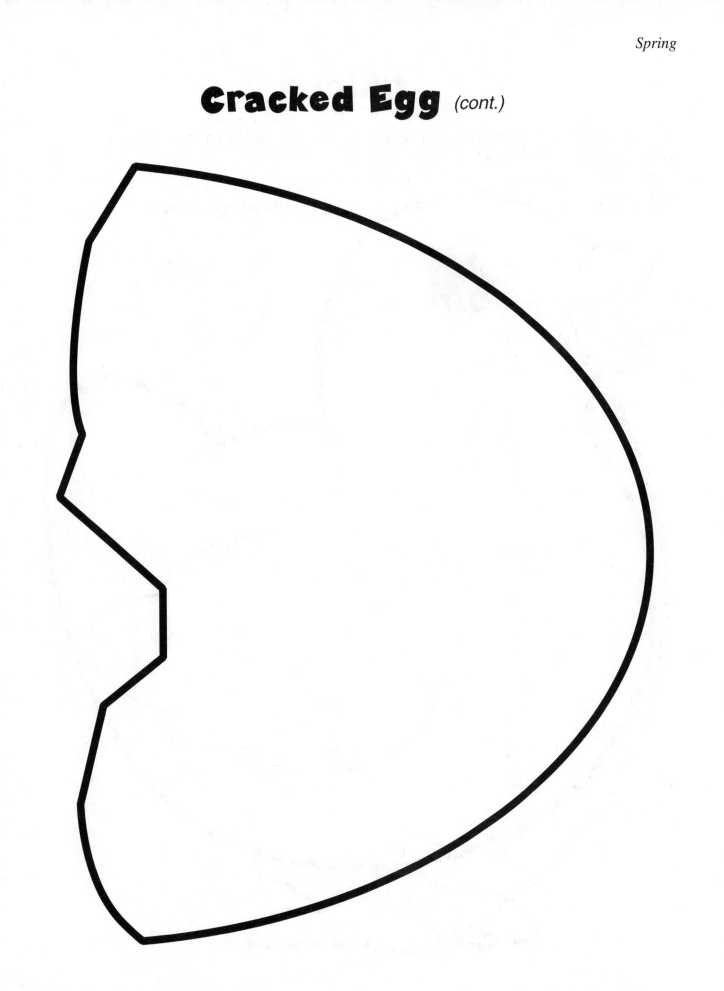

Chick

This chirping chick can stand on its own or nestle in the egg on page 138.

Robin

Use the robin with legs to stand near the nest on page 142, or cut nest on the dotted line and set the robin in the nest.

Nest and Eggs

Cut out eggs and arrange in nest. If they are robin's eggs, paint them blue! The robin is on page 141.

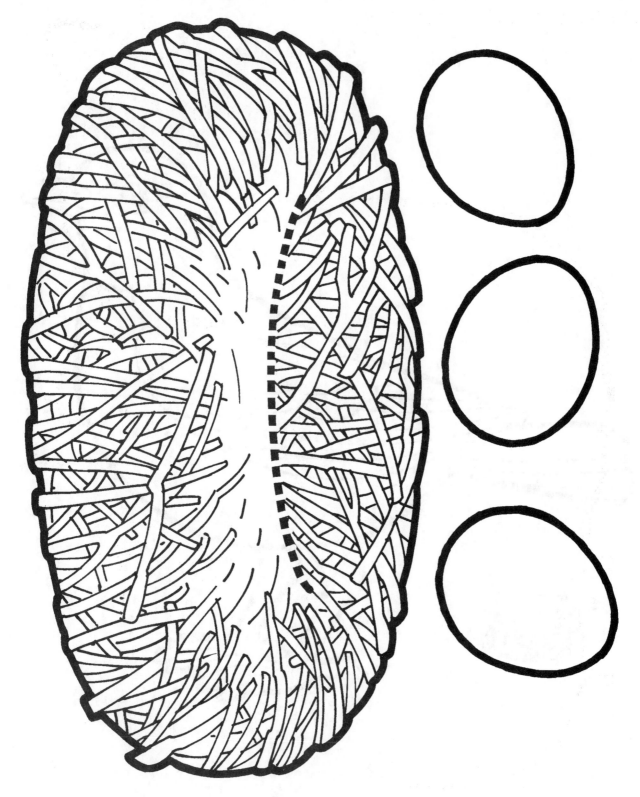

Spring Lamb

Use pages 143–144. Cut along the dotted lines to arrange the wreath around the lamb's neck. Attach the legs at tabs A, B, C, and D. Attach the tail with a brad.

A

B

C

D

Spring

Spring Lamb *(cont.)*

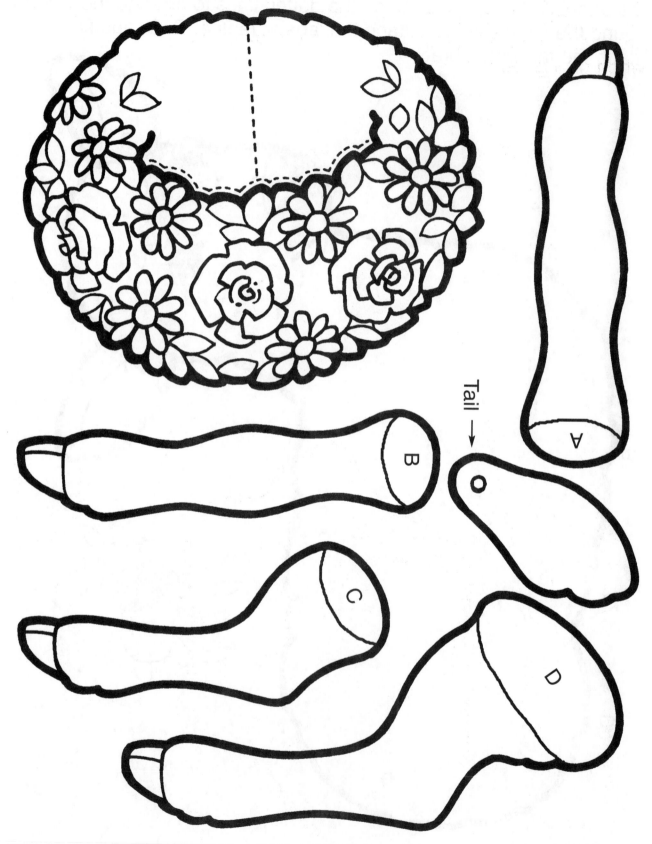

Tail →

A

B

C

D

O

Daffodil

Color and cut out daffodil pieces. View diagram for placement of flower parts. If you are not planning to place the daffodil on a piece of background paper, use sturdy paper and overlap stem and leaves when gluing together.

Tulip

Color and cut out tulip pieces. View diagram for placement of flower parts. If you are not planning to place the tulip on a background piece of paper, use sturdy paper and overlap stem and leaves when gluing together.

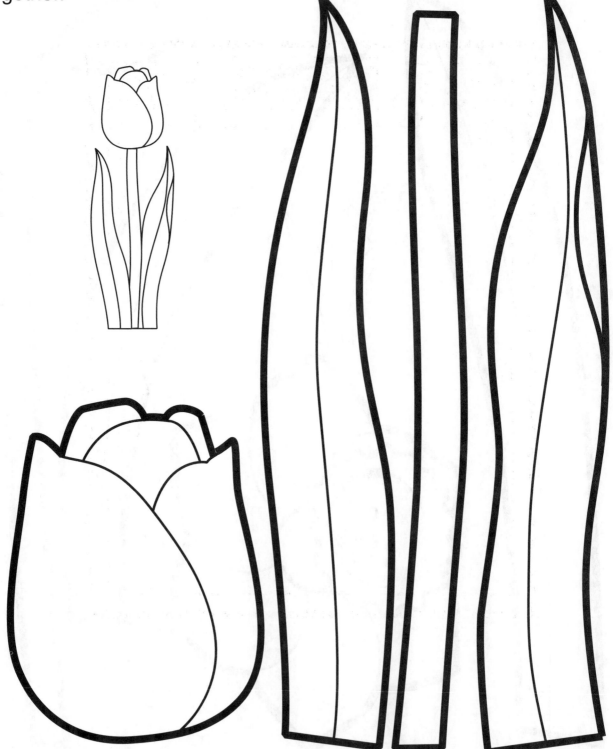

146

Seed Packet

Flower Pot

Use with flowers on page 145–146.

148

Beehive

Use pages 149–150

Bees

Inchworm

Use pages 151–152. Connect the large inchworm at the tab. The fully assembled inchworm will be one foot long. Combine the six small inchworms from each page on a twelve-inch strip of paper and make a ruler.

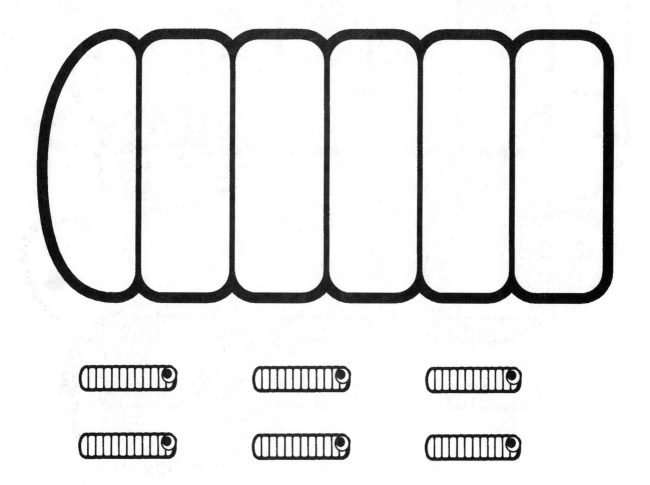

Inchworm *(cont.)*

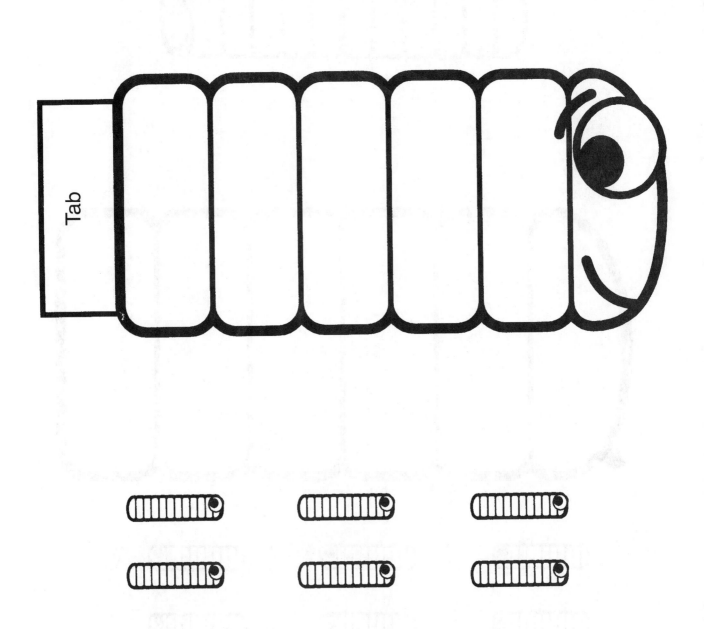

Butterfly

Use pages 153–155. Color and then cut out the pieces. Place a small amount of glue over the A on the body section. Attach the wings to the butterfly body by aligning the wings over A. Once attached, bend legs down.

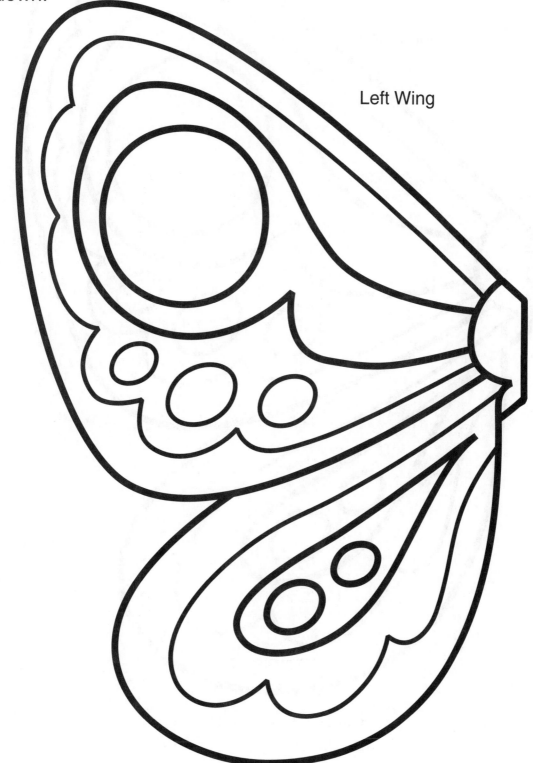

Left Wing

Butterfly *(cont.)*

Right Wing

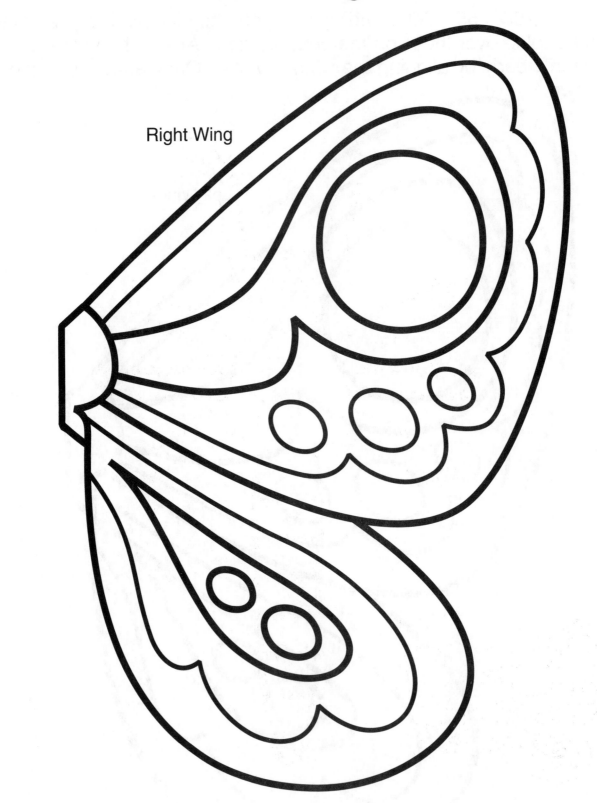

Butterfly *(cont.)*

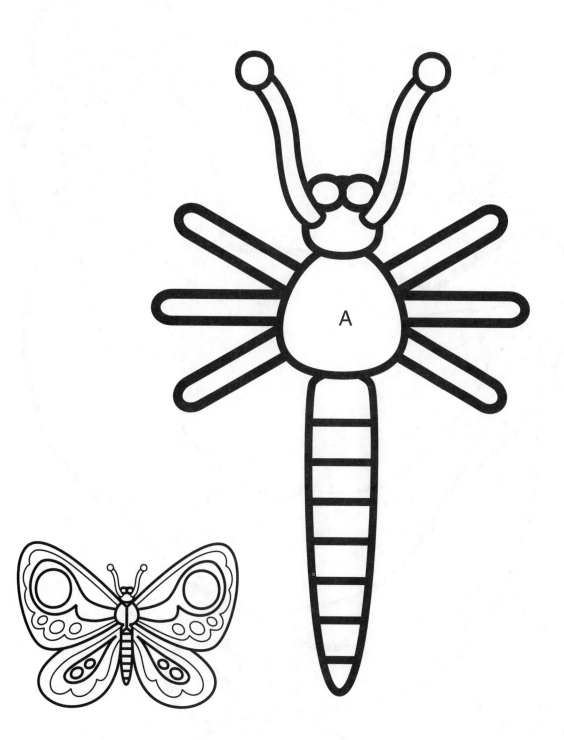

Hen and Chick

Pig and Piglet

Cow

158

Duck and Duckling

Horse

Barn

Use pages 161 and 162. Connect the barn at the tab. Cut barn doors on solid lines and fold back at dotted lines to open. Use the animals from pages 158–160 and the silo and the haystack on pages 163–164 to complete the farm scene.

Barn *(cont.)*

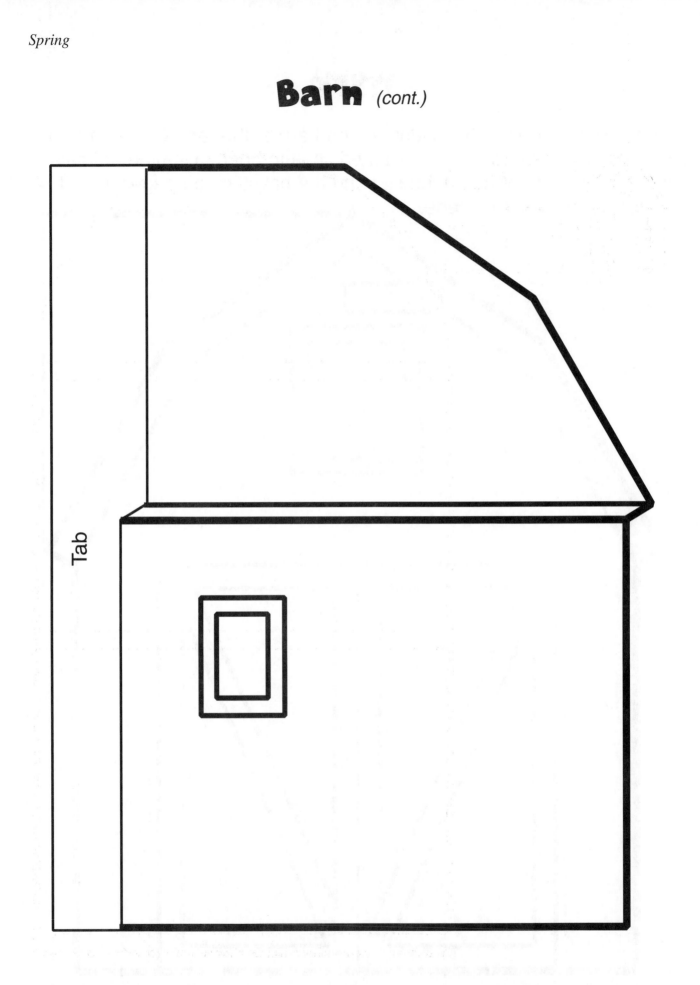

Silo

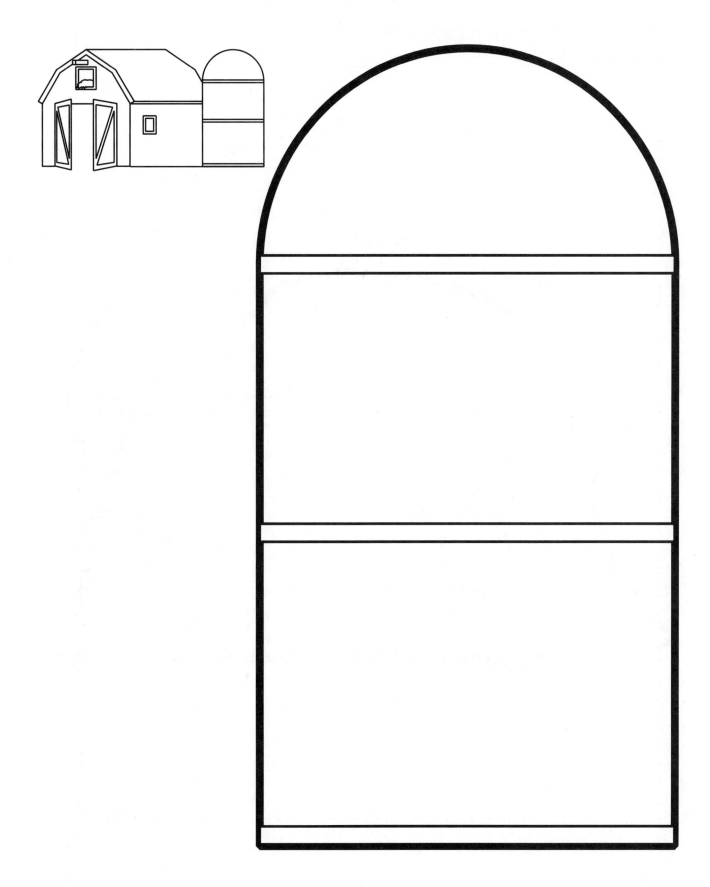

Hay Stack

Use with the barn on pages 161–163.

164

Kite

Use pages 165–166. Connect the kite at the tab.

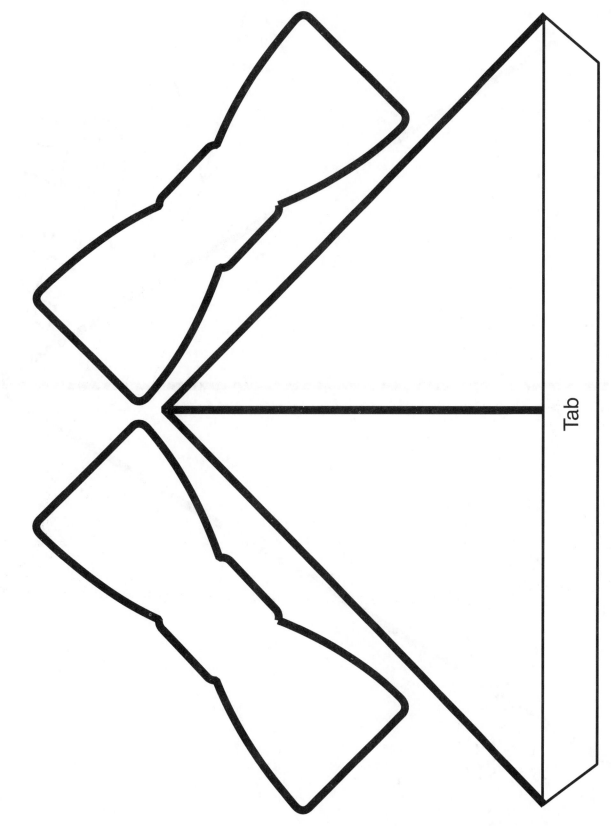

Kite *(cont.)*

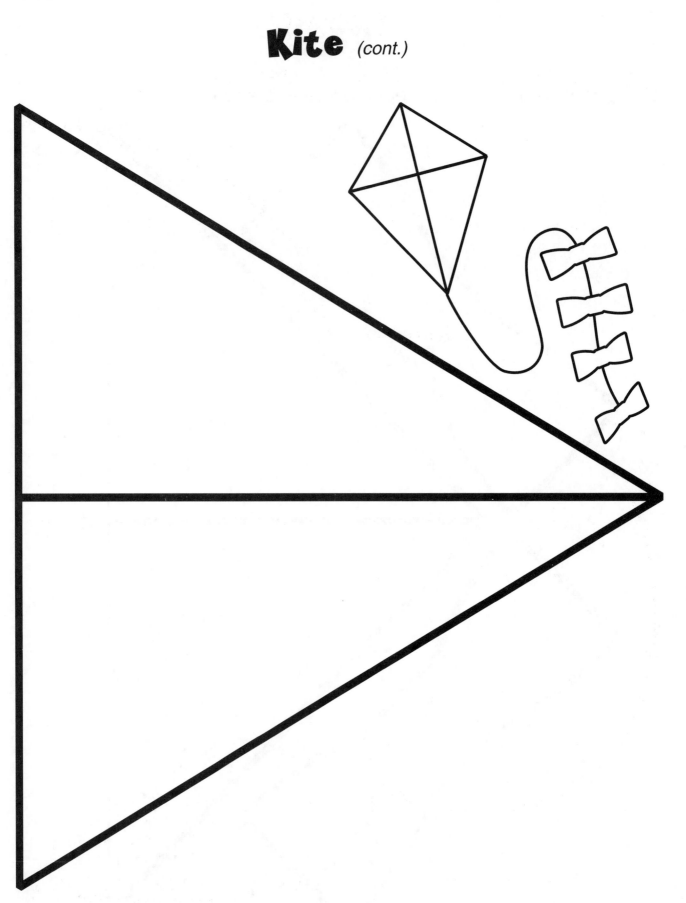

Cloud

Use pages 167–168. Connect the cloud at the tab.

Cloud *(cont.)*

Tab

Raindrops

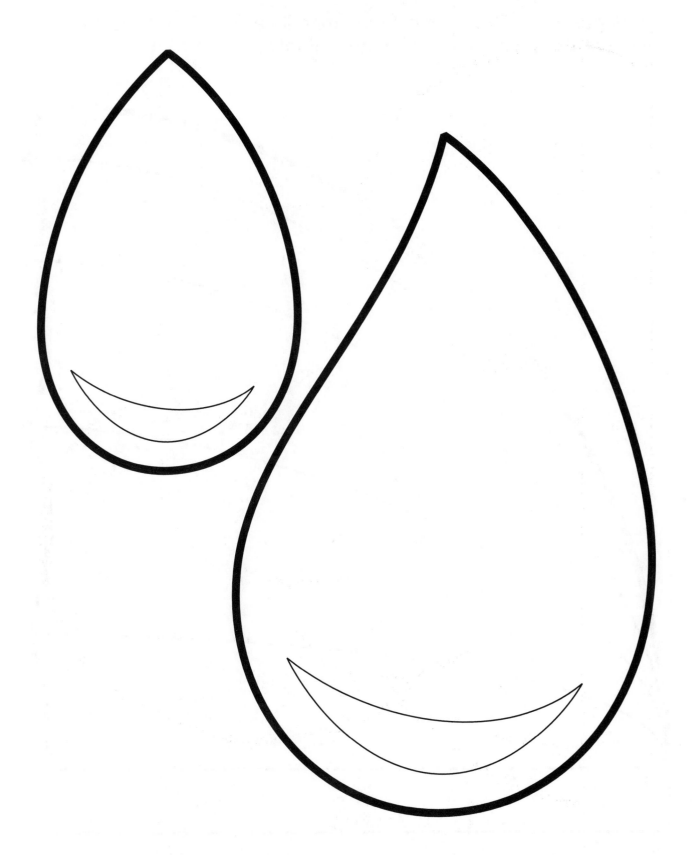

Umbrella

Use pages 170–172. Connect the umbrella at Tab A. Connect the handle at Tab B and attach it to the umbrella.

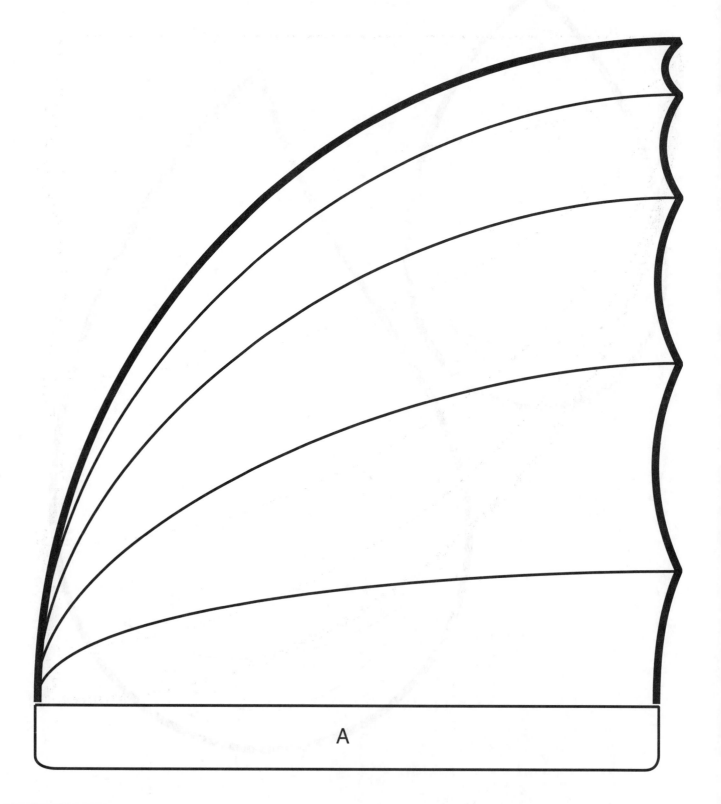

A

Umbrella *(cont.)*

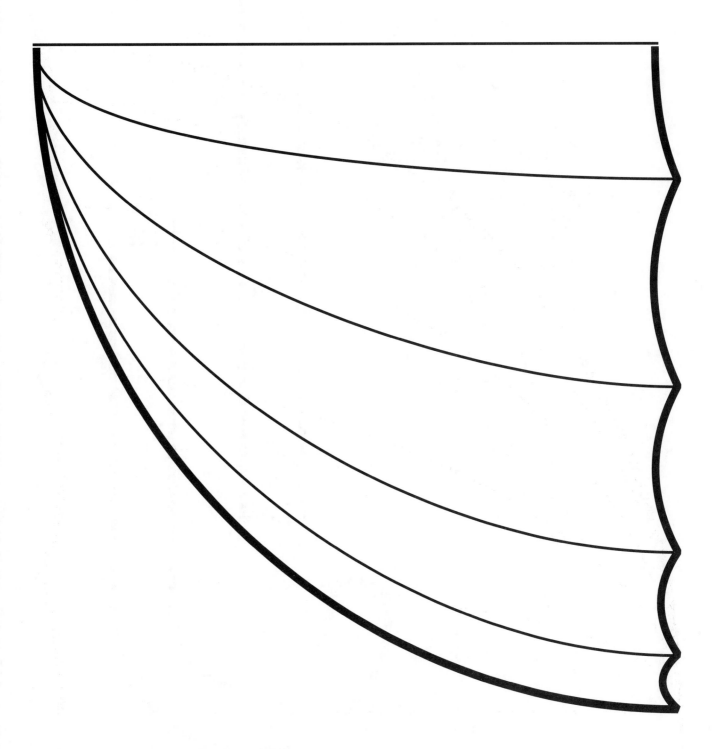

Umbrella *(cont.)*

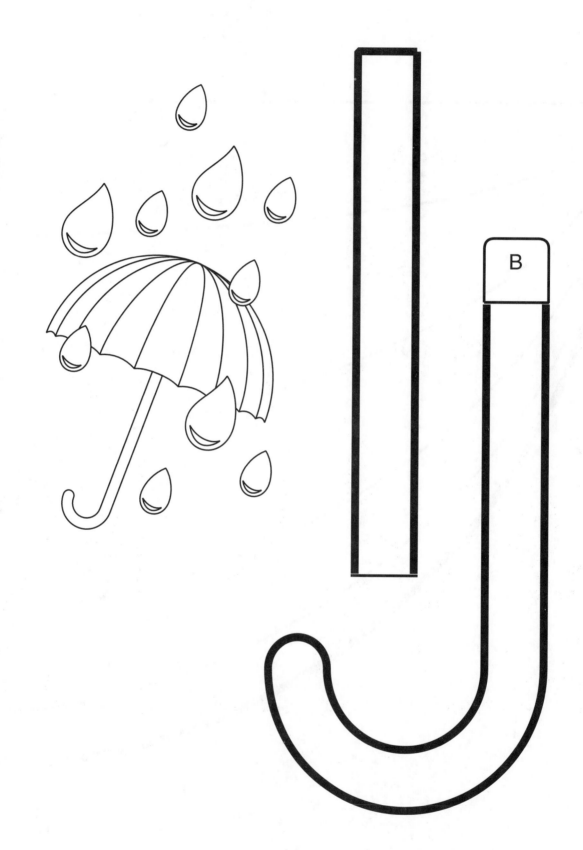

B

Small Bunnies

Easter Bunny

Use pages 174–176. Overlap the neck and attach it to Tab A. (You may wish to cut off the black line at the end of the neck.) Attach the tail at Tab B. Place the apron and then add the arms at C & D. Be careful to place the paintbrush before completely gluing down the arm.

Easter Bunny *(cont.)*

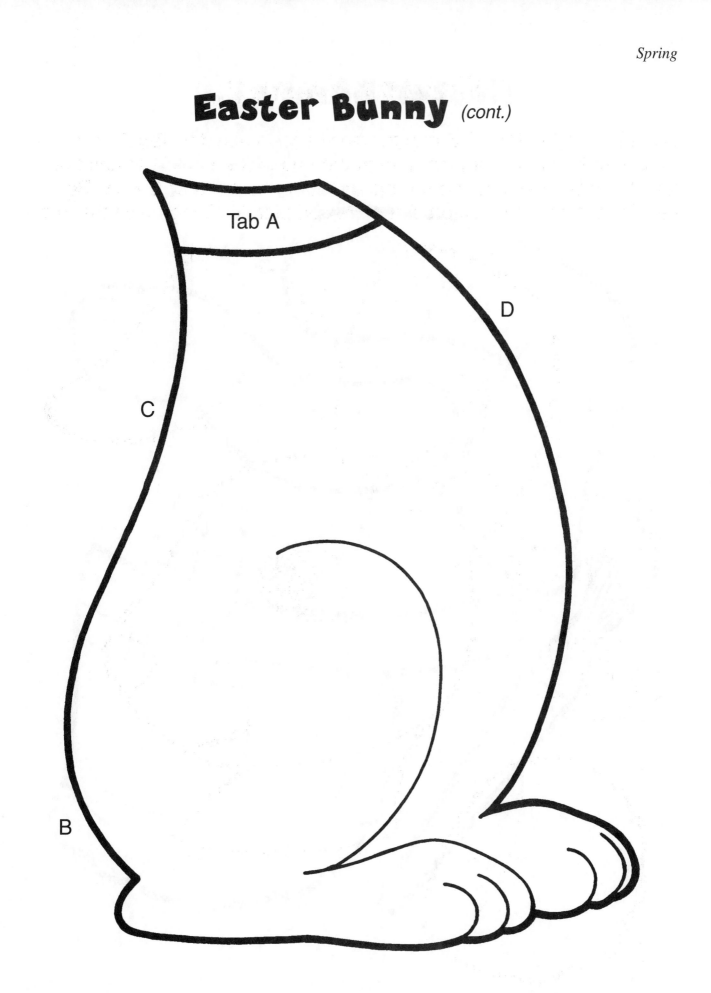

Tab A

D

C

B

Easter Bunny *(cont.)*

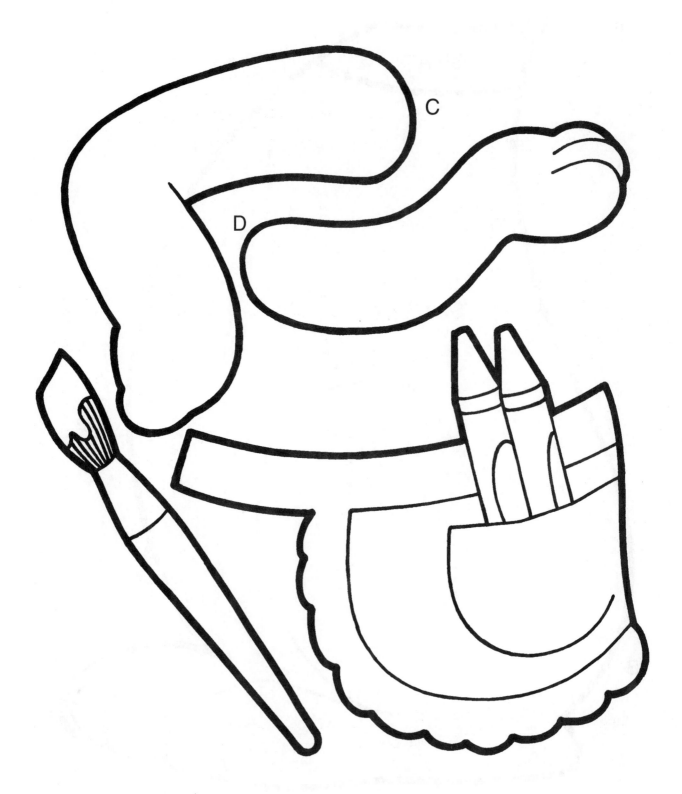

Paint Can and Brush

Plain Egg and Carrot

Bunny Ears and Eggs

Attach the ears to a headband or make a bunny using paper plates for the head and body and add the ears.

Easter Egg

Basket

Use pages 181–182. Connect the handle to the basket at A and B.
Attach the bow if desired and fill with colored eggs (page 179) or
flowers (pages 145, 146, and 190).

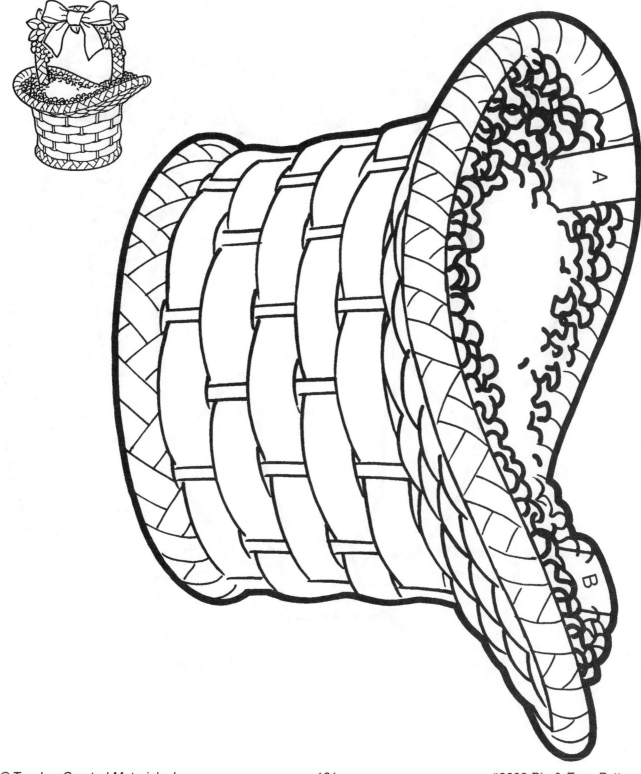

Basket *(cont.)*

A

B

I Love You, Mom

Rose

Color and cut out the rose pieces. View diagram for placement of flower parts. If you are not planning to place the rose on a piece of background paper, use sturdy paper and overlap stem and leaves when gluing together.

Bow

I Love You, Dad

Tie

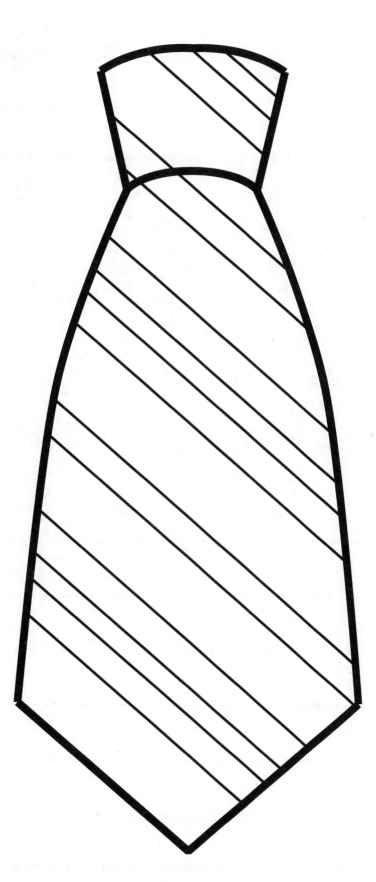

American Flag

Use pages 188–189.

Connect the flag at the tab.

American Flag *(cont.)*

Tab

Poppy

Color and cut out the poppy pieces. View diagram for placement of flower parts. If you are not planning to place the poppy on a piece of background paper, copy onto sturdy paper and overlap stem and leaves when gluing together.

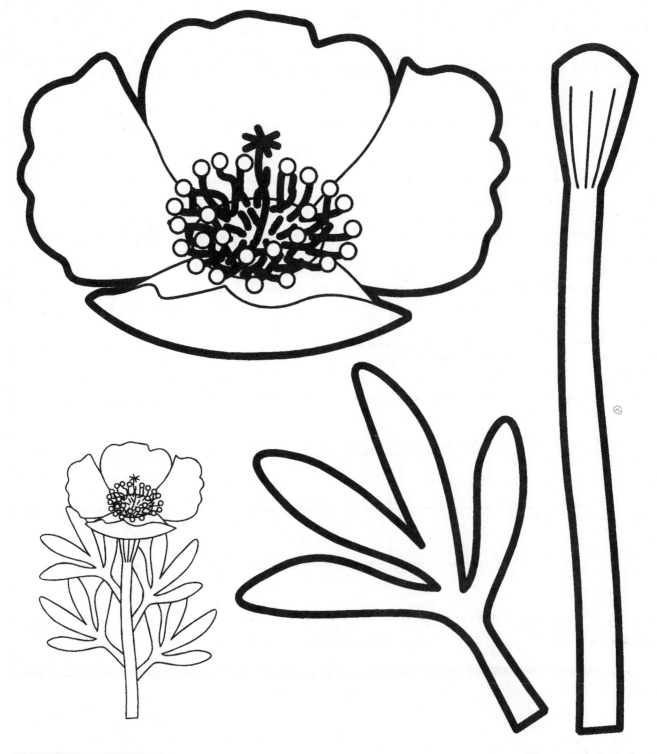

Summer Patterns and Ideas

Use the sun pattern to make a stuffed paper sculpture or to decorate your summer bulletin board. Enlarge the sun diagram to create math manipulatives or calendar shapes. Use the other weather symbols, such as the cloud, the raindrops, and the snowflake with the sun to graph the weather.

Stretch blue crepe paper streamers across the length of the bulletin board and use the sea life patterns to create an ocean habitat. Suspend sea gulls from the ceiling with fishing line.

Shovels and pails, seashells, and hot dogs and buns can be used in the math center. Write a number on each shell pattern and place real shells in the center. Have students place the appropriate number of shells on the pattern. Use math facts, story questions, or counting activities to match the shovel with the right pail. Make several copies of the fish pattern and use them to make up math stories involving addition and subtraction.

Write a fish poem or story in a Fish Shape Book. The starfish pattern can be a lacing card, a bingo card, or a shape book.

Run the sunflower head on brown paper, the petals on yellow paper, and the leaves on green paper. Have students glue the flower head to cardstock or a piece of manila folder and cut it out. Cover the brown paper with glue and sprinkle on sunflower seeds. Glue yellow petals to the outside edge. Paint a wooden stir stick or ruler green and glue on the leaves and the flower head.

Use the swim trunks and swimsuit patterns to create Swimming Big Books. Discuss water safety. Use the snorkel, mask, and fin patterns as story props or in the Drama Center. Make up a class story about a deep sea adventure and record it in a big book.

Have students color and cut out sunglasses. Cut out the lenses and stretch colored plastic wrap over the openings. Secure with tape or glue. Decorate glasses with sequins or glitter and attach the sides. Write clues on footsteps and hide them around the room to create a scavenger hunt, or use as nonstandard measurement tools or flashcards.

Run the ice cream cone on brown paper and the ice cream on several different colored papers. Have students build an ice cream cone as an art project or laminate the pieces to use as a game in your math center. Write a numeral on each cone and have students build ice cream cones with the correct number of scoops of ice cream. Use the scoops of ice cream as a motivational tool—when the class reaches certain goal, they get an ice cream party! Chart their progress with the scoops. Build a Favorite Flavors Graph by labeling cones across the bottom of the graph with flavors and stacking scoops in the appropriate place as you poll the class.

Have students color, cut out, and assemble fireworks pattern. Use glue to trace over lines and sprinkle with a variety of colors of glitter. Use the flag pattern to discuss Independence Day.

Use the autograph album pattern as a cover for individual albums. Allow students time to collect autographs of their classmates. Be sure to sign each album yourself!

Sun

Use pages 192–195. The four-page sun pattern is put together in a circular fashion.

Attach Tab A. It becomes the upper left quadrant. The sun section marked by Tab B becomes the lower left quadrant. Next, attach the sun section marked with Tab C at the lower right quadrant. Finally, place the quadrant marked with Tab D in the remaining space to complete the sun.

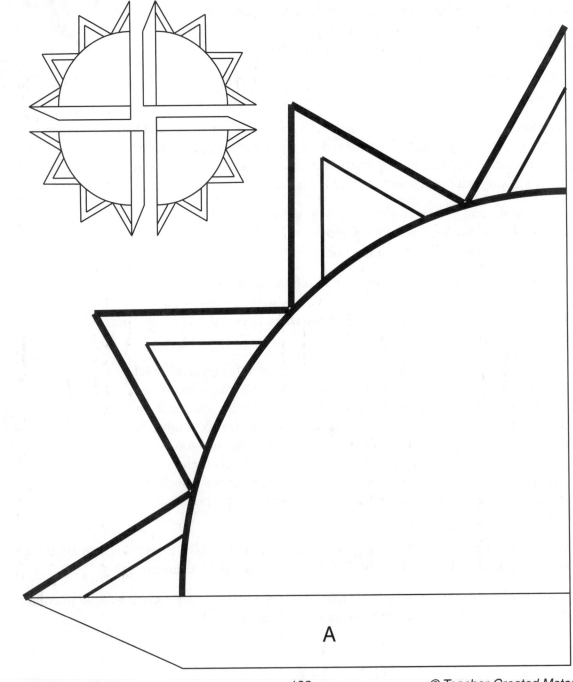

A

Sun *(cont.)*

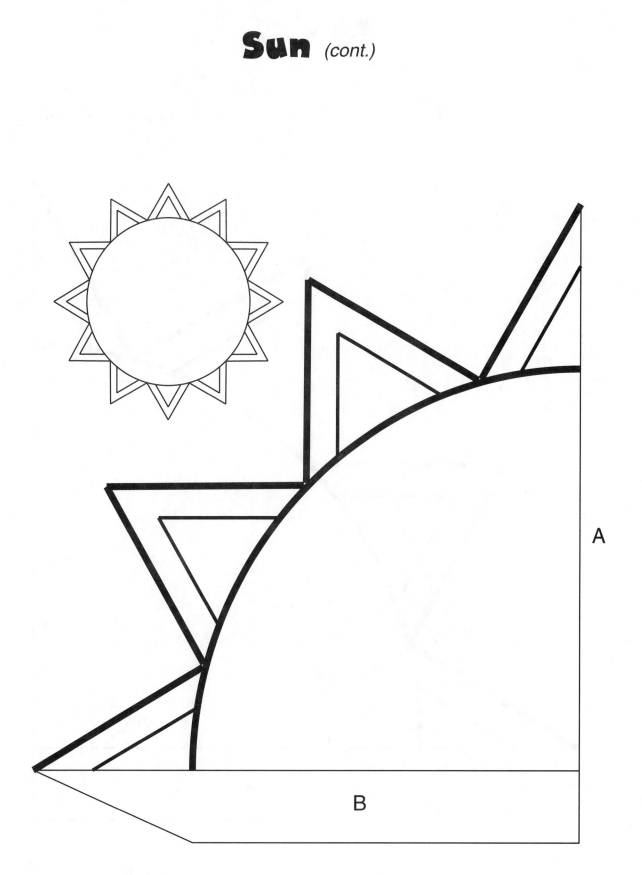

A

B

Sun *(cont.)*

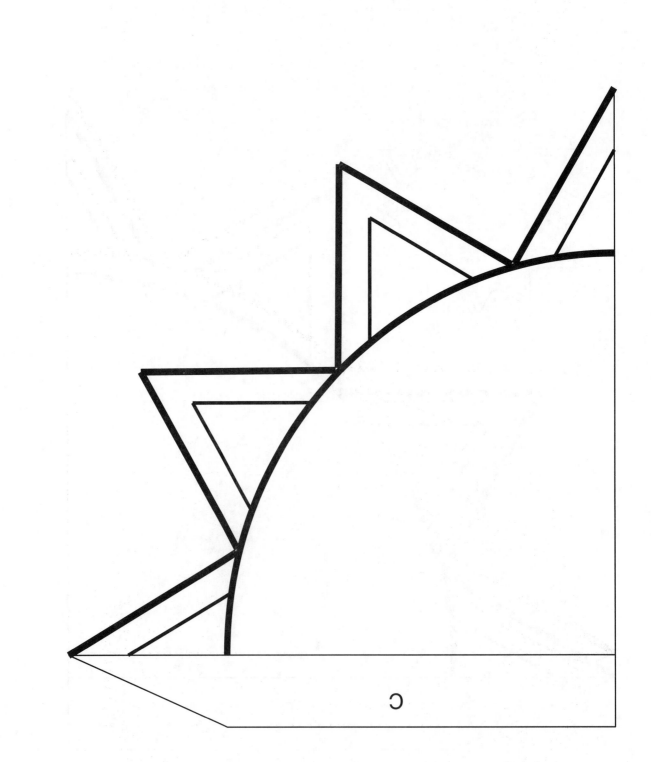

C

194

Sun *(cont.)*

D

Sea Horse

Sea Shells

Starfish

Fish

Tropical Fish

Seagull

Use pages 201–203. Attach the right wing at Tab A and the left wing at Tab B.

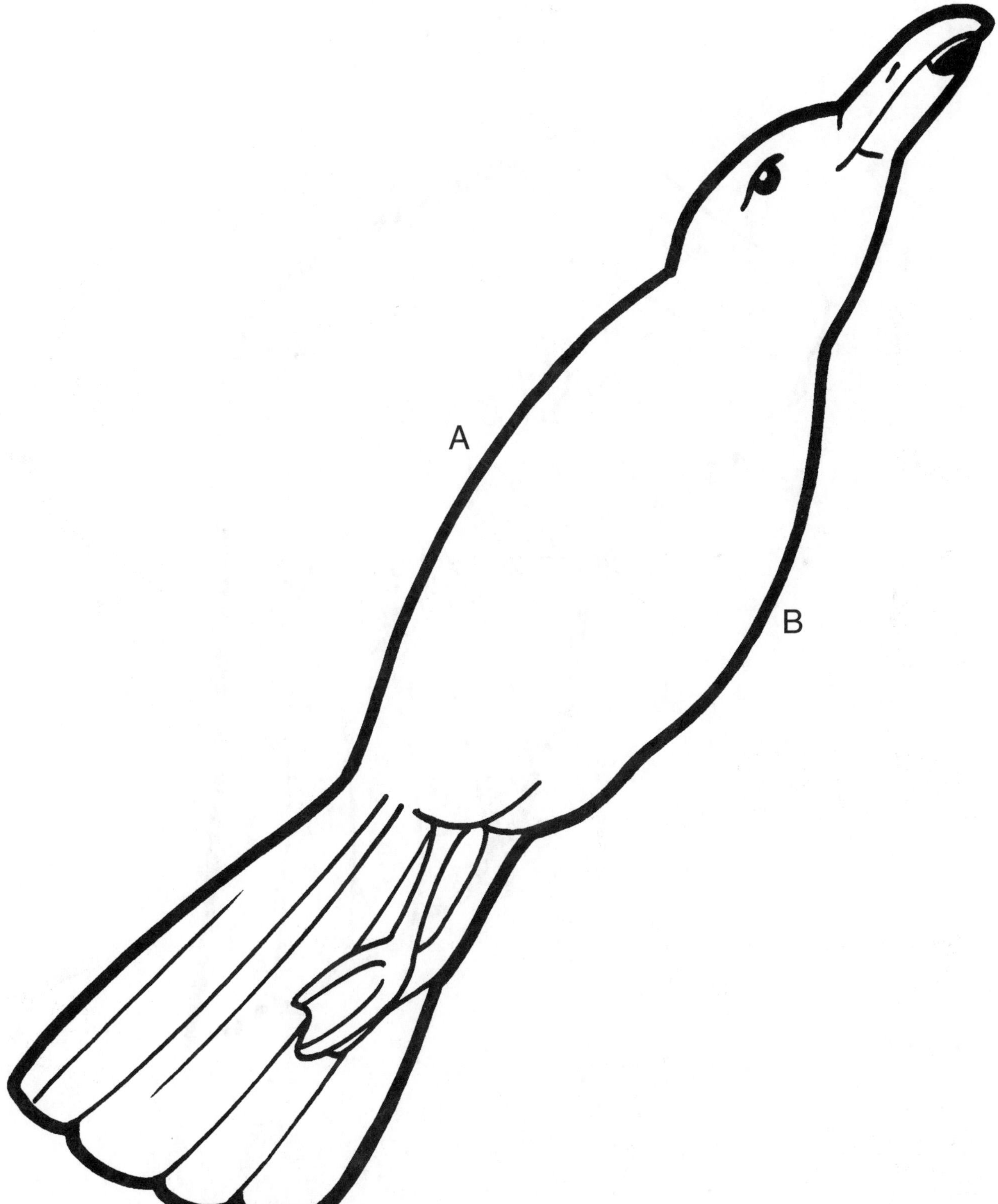

A

B

Seagull *(cont.)*

Tab B

Seagull *(cont.)*

Tab A

Crab

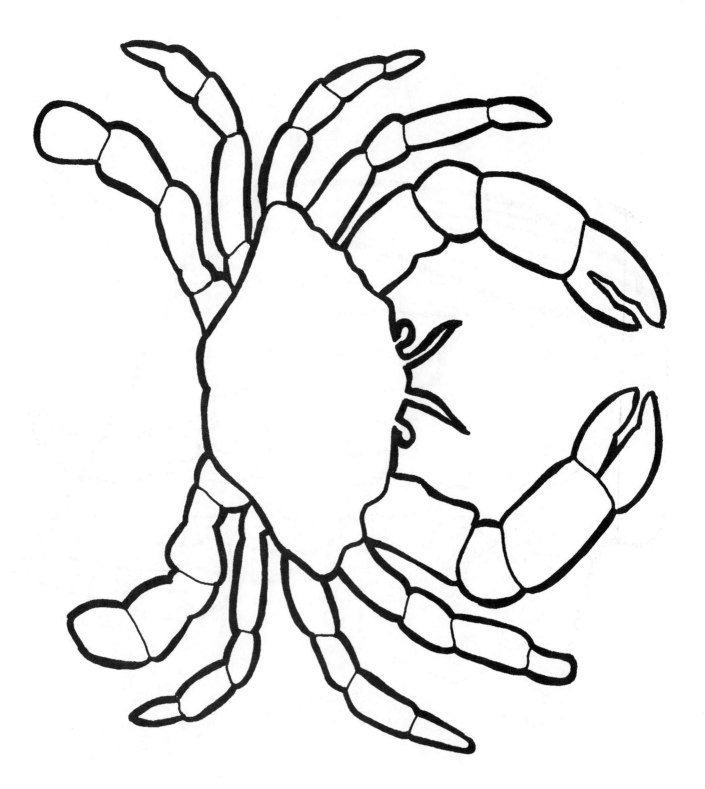

Octopus

Use pages 205–206. Connect the octopus at the tab.

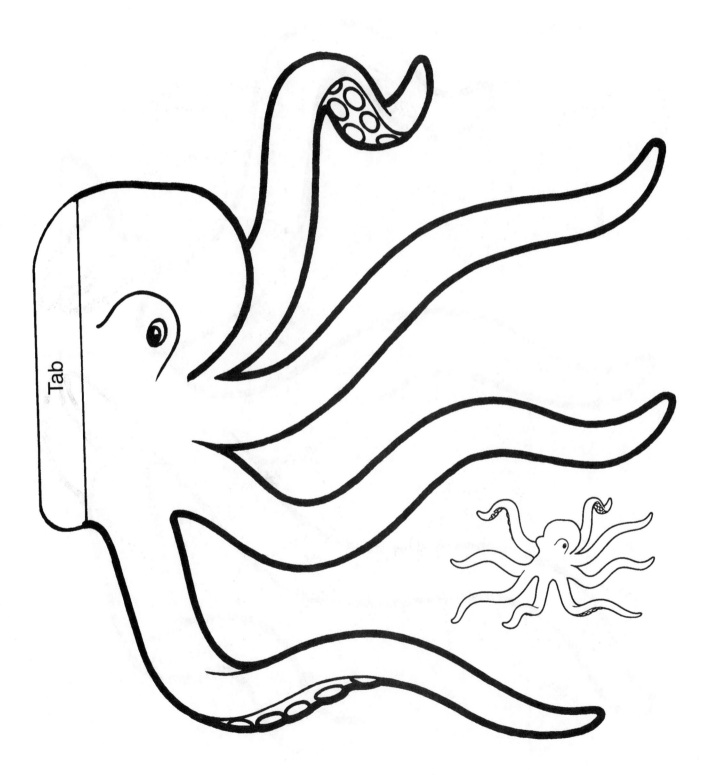

Octopus *(cont.)*

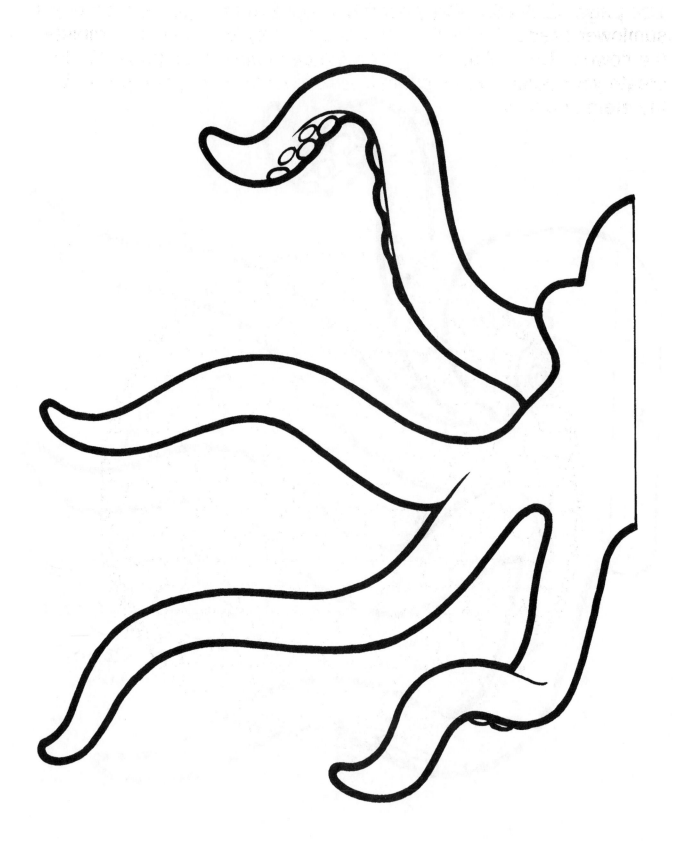

Sunflower

Use pages 207–208. Copy seed head on brown paper and cover with sunflower seeds. You will need approximately 25 petals to complete the flower. Use yellow paper and the petal pattern on page 208 to create your petals. Paint a small stick green or use green paper for the stem and leaves.

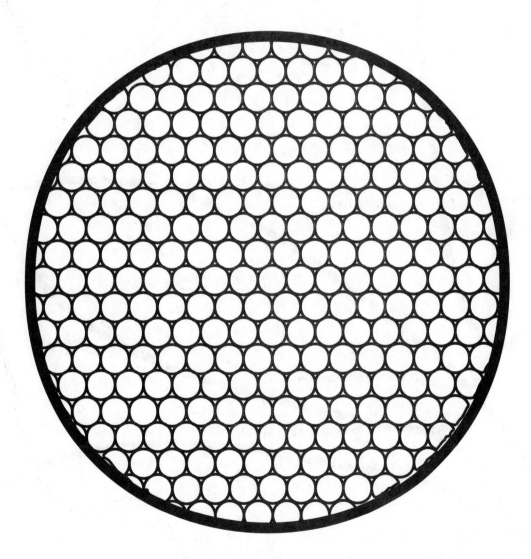

Sunflower *(cont.)*

Swim Trunks

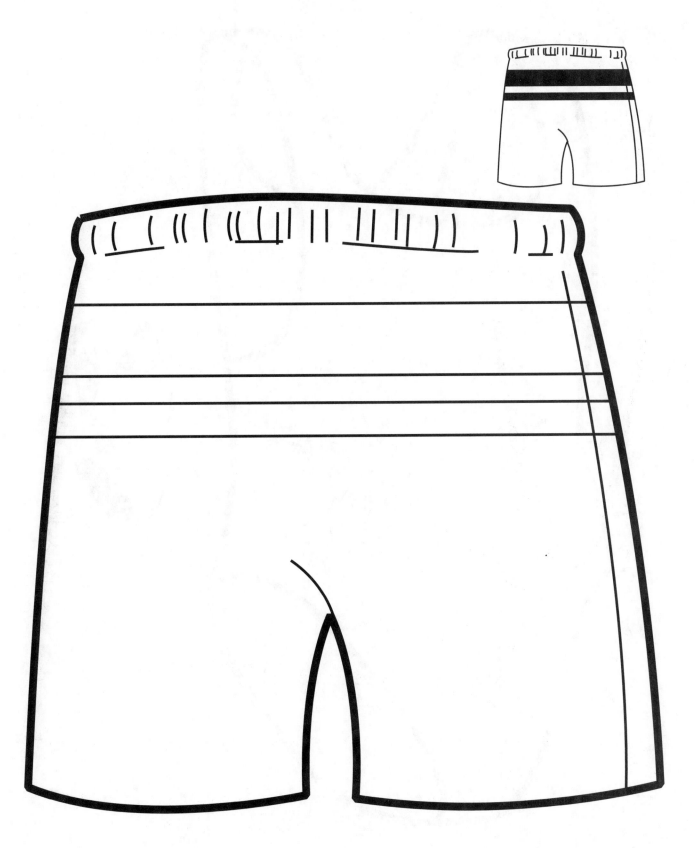

Swimsuit

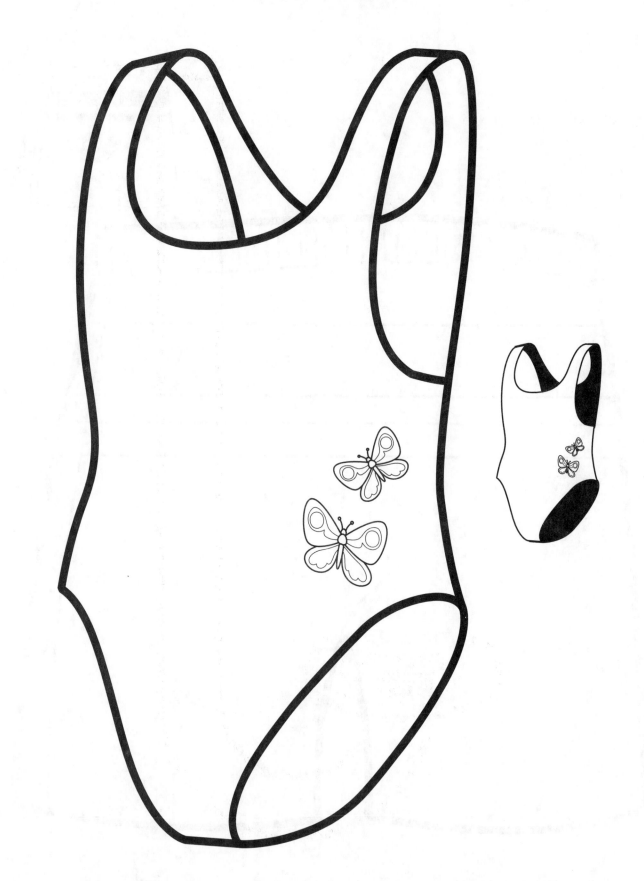

Snorkel

FinS

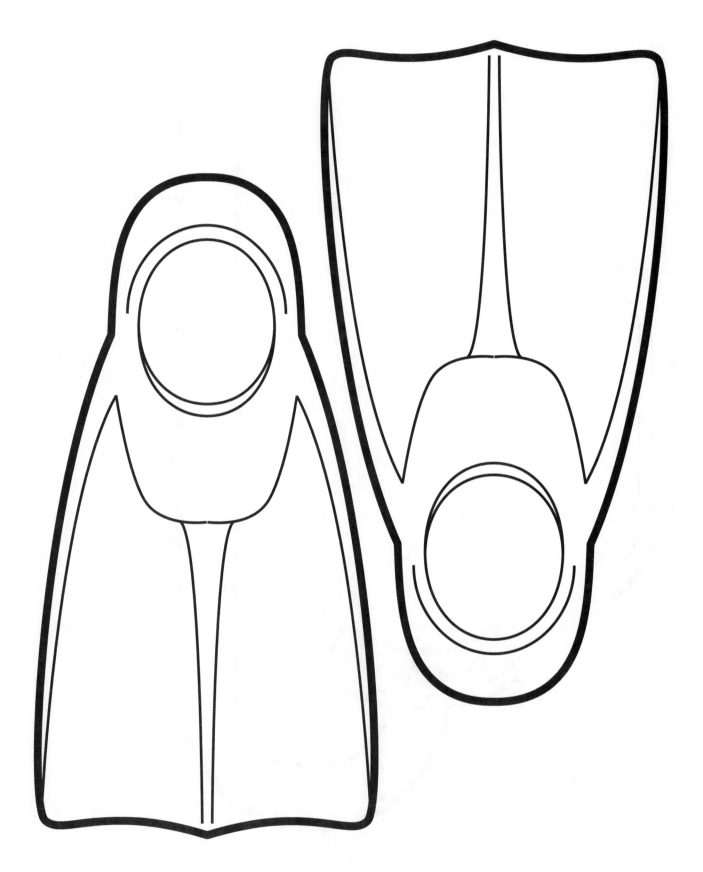

212

Mask

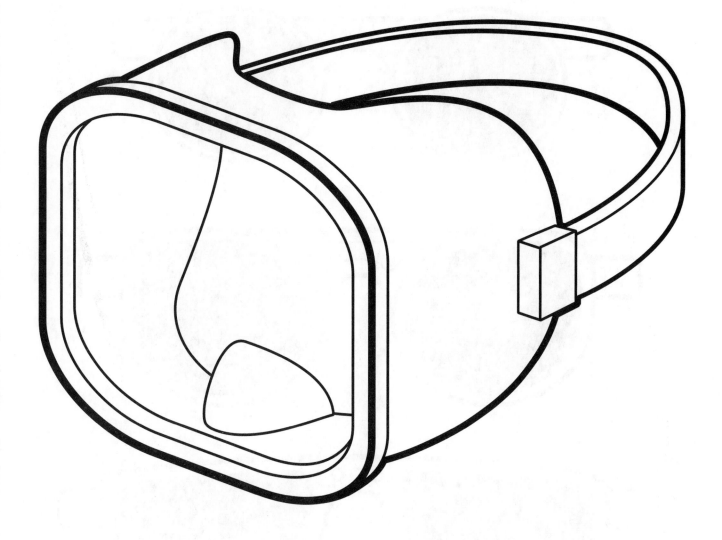

Sunglasses

Use pages 214–215. Bend tabs at the end of the lenses and attach sides. (See diagram on page 215.)

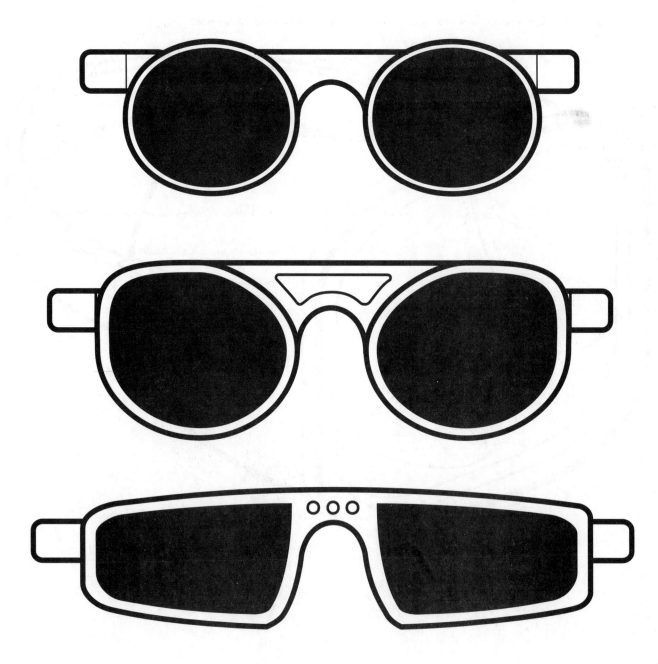

Sunglasses *(cont.)*

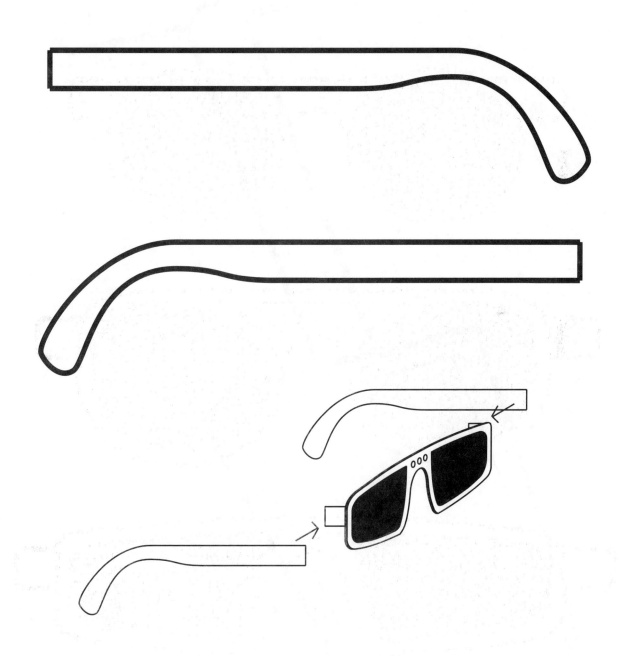

Sand Shovel

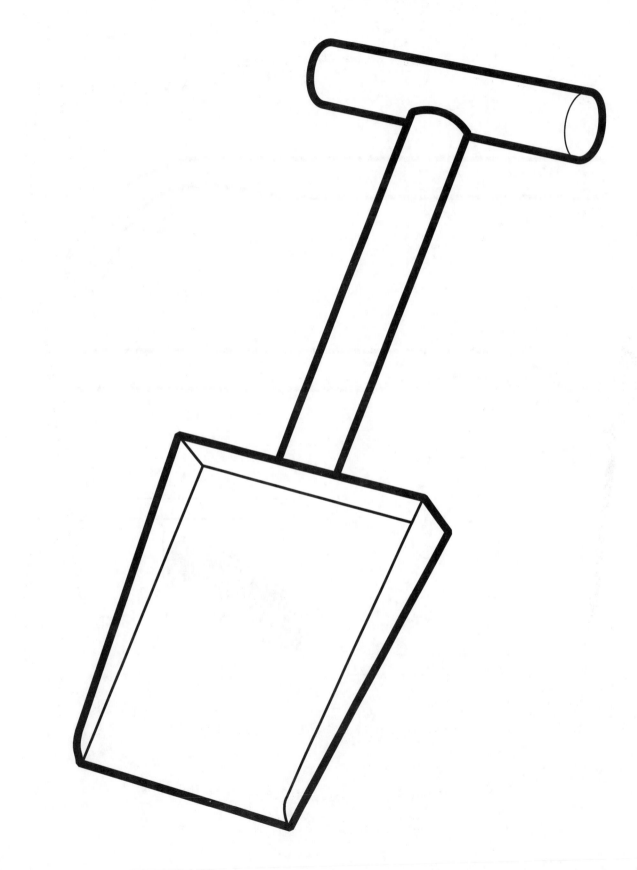

216   *© Teacher Created Materials, Inc.*

Sand Pail

Footprints

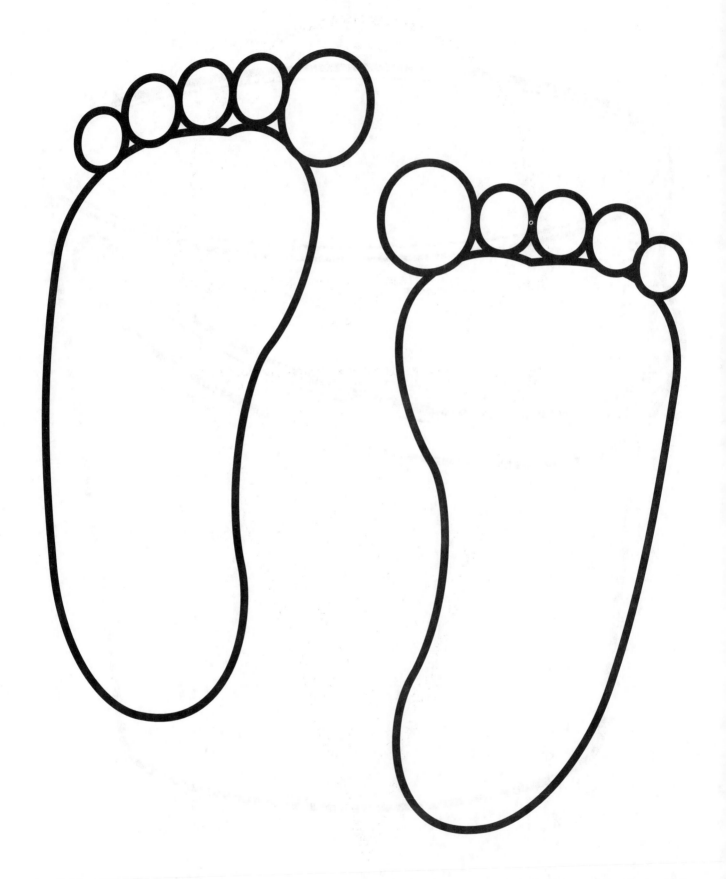

Ice Cream Cone

Ice Cream Scooper

Fireworks

Use pages 222–223. Connect to the tab. Decorate with glitter.

Fireworks *(cont.)*

Tab A

222

Hot Dog

Cut a slit in the bun on the dotted line to slip in the hot dog. Glue on red and yellow yarn for ketchup and mustard.

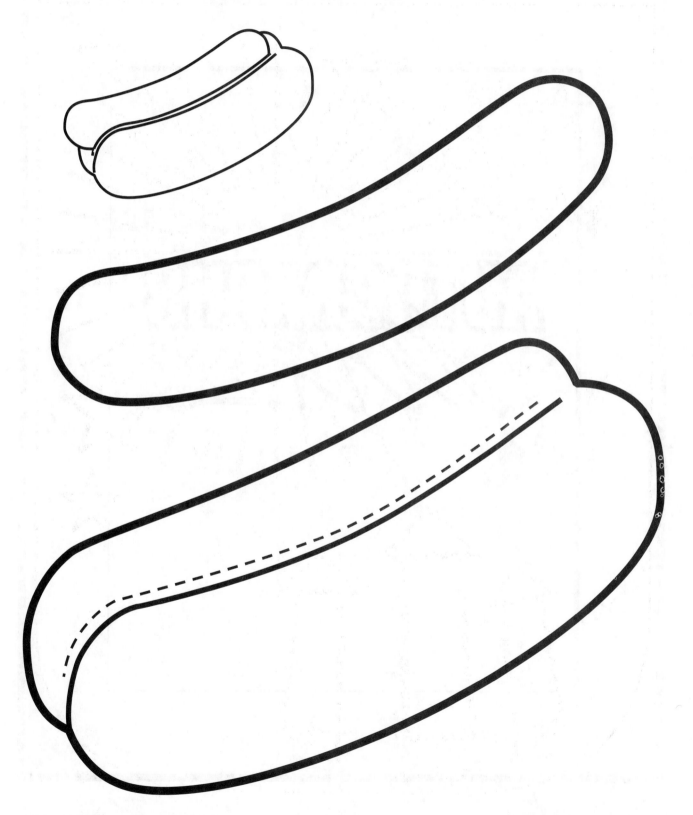

223   *#2602 Big & Easy Patterns*

Autograph Album